South of the County, *New Myths and Tales*
by South Dublin Writers
Guest Writer Geraldine Mills
Edited by Eileen Casey
Published by Fiery Arrow Press

Supported by EBS Community Fund
South Dublin County Libraries

South of the County
An Anthology of New Myths and Tales

Published by Fiery Arrow Press
16, Watermeadow Park,
Old Bawn
Tallaght, Dublin 24.

        all rights reserved.
No part of this publication may be reproduced in any form or by any means without the prior permission of the publisher.

Copyright remains with each individual author

Cover images courtesy of Jim Fitzpatrick

First published November, 2010

ISBN 978-0-9552237-1-6

South of the County
An Anthology of New Myths and Tales

The Spear of Lugh, Tallaght Village, 2010

P.no	Title	Author
7	Introduction	Eileen Casey
11	Between Worlds	Geraldine Mills
17	Wolves	David Mohan
29	Cittie's Cure	Niamh Bagnell
36	The Spear of Lugh	Eileen Casey
39	Dead Lives	Brian Kirk
43	Hell Fire Club	Julie Coombes Kiernan
46	Journey's End	Marie Gahan
50	Killinardan	Tom Myp
53	Lord Ballyowen's Legacy	Triona Walsh
60	The Celtic Cat	Susan Condon
68	Ares, Greek God of War	Martin Shannon
70	Red Sky	Victoria Mullen
74	River of Death	Joe McKiernan
79	Saved by the Bell	Ailish Massey
83	Small Gods in the Trees	Colm Keegan
93	Love Potion	Genevieve Greene
97	Send for the Swans	Aine Lyons
99	Silver Willow	Patricia Verdon
104	Snowdrop	Louise Phillips
111	The Sweet Breath of Deception	Joan Power
116	Tallaght Deer and the Goddess Ceres	Grace Moore
118	The Black Plague	Robert Dowdall
122	The Gift of Dance	Ann Cullen
125	The Hermitage	Mae Newman
129	Secrets of the Tower	Betty Keogh
133	Round Rower	Doreen Duffy
137	Croinin, the Celtic Tree of Knowledge	Veronica O'Neil

139	Weeping Willow	Joan Byrne
143	The Wrath of Plagerous	Brigid Flynn
147	Hidden	Vivienne Kearns
151	From Sherwood to Kingswood	Jim Archer
155	Hera	Maeve Murphy
160	Contributors' Notes	
170	Acknowledgements	

Introduction

Although cultures all over the globe have their own unique store of myths and fairytales, there is a common unifying thread. We use these narrative devices to try to answer fundamental questions which strive to explain the workings of the world itself and account for our presence in it. We can confront our 'demons' concerning our connection with time and place, invoke gods and goddesses, imbue frail humankind with noble and heroic deeds. This challenge inevitably evokes a questioning of our environment and how best to preserve it.

One of my favourite films is *Pan's Labyrinth* (Guillermo Del Toro) mainly because it interweaves fantasy with stark reality in a way that tries to negotiate interconnecting spaces between the physical and the imaginative. These surreal spaces are bridges towards reaching the portals of other dimensions.

It seems fitting that the idea for an anthology of stories which lean towards mythology and folklore should come from a landscape source such as Tallaght. This New Town, birthed from a place of sacred history, has a mystical treasury of mountain and stream, mauve hazy layers of heather on the Dublin Mountains, flocks of wild birds, swans, herons, kingfishers and kestrels. Tallaght also evokes so many place names full of mystery and reverence. Place names like Ballinascorney, Town of the Gorge, Kiltipper, The Church of the Well, Brittas, The Speckled Land, Lugmore, The Great Hollow and

Tymon derived from O'Mothan's inheritance. There's a vibrant awareness and nurturing of local history in Tallaght, due in no small measure to the continuing work of Tallaght Historical Society. Also, there is an extensive Local Studies archive in Tallaght Library. In March, 2010, Eamonn Maloney's *Tallaght, a place with history*, came as a welcome and valuable addition to this store. The myths and tales in this anthology are inspired by well known areas in South Dublin such as Citywest, Griffeen Valley, Clondalkin, Lucan, Gleann na Smole, Rathfarnham Castle, and many others. Readers of this publication will enjoy tracing their own unique connection to these placenames and 'reading' them through the lens of each individual writer's vision.

The idea to bring together this rich and diverse material happened one day, while I was walking through Tallaght Village. I noticed a spear shaped rooftop piercing upwards towards the morning sky. The Tuatha De Danann came to my mind, especially their many magical traits and magical possessions. The four best known are Dagda's Cauldron, The Spear of Lugh, The Stone of Fal and Nuada's Sword of Light. This great pre-Christian tribe were gods and goddesses, their first battles were on the West Coast but soon they had defeated the Fir Bolg and their power spread quickly.

That 'one day' story took root in my mind, one which marries the ancient past with the modern present. The resulting narrative 'The Spear of Lugh' soon helped me realise that contemporary mythology is a rich source of connection with the landscape in spiritual, environmental, historical and mythological ways. I then invited the writers included here to interpret South Dublin landscape also in this way. Their response proved awe inspiring.

This anthology brings together writers from all over South Dublin. Their achievements are many, these writers are rapidly making names for themselves on a national and international basis. Such is the generosity of spirit in the County that 'the rising boat lifts all tides' is never more appropriate. Included here is Galway writer Geraldine Mills who lived in Tallaght under the shelter of the Dublin Mountains for fifteen years and was a founder member of St Colmcilles' Writing Group in the 1980's. Geraldine is the Sunday Tribune/Hennessy Award winner (fiction), 2000, an achievement which also came to Lucan writer David Mohan (poetry) in 2008.

It is an enormous privilege to have the work of so many South Dublin writers under one 'sky' as it were, writers at various stages of their writing journey united in providing a shining new key to opening those portals within us which encourage a nurturing bond with the place where we live.

I wish to acknowledge the support of The EBS Community Fund and South Dublin County Libraries, without which this publication would not have been possible.

Eileen Casey

Palu

Between Worlds

I come upon him in the fruit and veg aisle. A remnant from Electric Picnic is my guess, what with the long, tangled hair and beard, leather boots, the blanket thingy thrown across his shoulder. He's gnawing on a carrot like he has one serious attack of the munchies. I turn the corner and there he is again in the tinned food section. People are dancing their way around him with their trolleys, children pulling at cans of beans and spaghetti hoops and crashing them down on top of soft sliced pans, moshing them. He's standing there with a John West salmon in his hand, pressing his thumb against the label, putting it to his mouth. Somewhere above the clatter and squeak of trolleys, a disembodied voice is telling us that there are special offers on tanning lotion.

He's biting into a triple 'A' battery as I make my way towards the till. Then I hear, 'help me, please'. I do a double take and point to my good self. "Moi? "

'Am I in hell or what?' he whispers.

'Well, people have been known to call it that on a Friday night but…'

'I have to get out of here, back to Seefin. Some of my men… I must get back to see if they're alive.'

It's then I notice the scratches on his face, his arms. I see blood on his hands. He's been in the wars all right. I don't know what happens next but I find myself at the checkout, paying for his tins of salmon and putting them in my bag with my quarter pound of mince, my dinners for one. When we get out into the

fresh air he's like a dog with his first porcupine he's so surprised. He manoeuvres himself gingerly around the cars and when he sees the Luas go by he has conniptions, starts swinging his sword at the monster snake. I distract him with a bar or two of *More than a Woman* and we walk across the bridge, me still singing. Mothers pushing buggies stare at us; teenagers carrying their bicycles down the steps take no notice. The sun's beginning to give up on the day.
'I'm Tara, by the way.'
'Finn,' he says.
'Oh, cool.'
'No Mac. MacCumhaill.'
Surely, he can't be serious.
Mary Stephens is out weeding her little patch as we turn into the estate. She's as good as Sky news and I know that before I have the code punched into the alarm, the whole road'll be wise to my business. Lucky greets us at the door, his black and white head bobbing in delight, his tail wagging. I take my cue from this little dog. He's my man barometer. When Finn kneels down to rub him, the dog starts licking his hand straight away.
'Lucky's giving you the OK,' I say happily. I relax.
It takes all of five minutes for the phone to ring. It's Mags.
'Please, don't tell me that's the dodgy guy from the speed dating night in there with you?'
'No, it's not. He's just a bit lost that's…'
'Aren't we all? You must be out of your tree. Did the last fiasco not teach you anything? You'll end up on

the front page of the Star, Garda tape all around the house, TV cameras; the lot.'
'You're being a tad melodramatic Mags.' 'Well, don't come whinging to me if you're found dismembered at the end of the garden.' She bangs down the phone.
'With friends like that,' I say to him, pointing at the receiver. 'Why are you talking to a funny bone?' he wonders. I laugh, funny bone, that's a good one. I bring him into the sitting room. 'I will light your fire,' he says, looking into my eyes. His are a welkin blue. Oh, crap. Mags was right, Lucky wrong. But no. Before you can say *Desperate Housewives*, he's taking two pieces of flint from his boot, striking them and has flames roaring up the chimney in no time. '
'Like home,' he says.
When I come back with the dinner, don't I find him fast asleep on the floor, the sheepskin rug that me and Jimmy fought over in the divorce, wrapped around him. I'm a sucker for men when they're asleep; they look so... so manageable. I give a little cough and he sits up with a start, goes immediately to his sword.
'Don't worry,' I say quietly, 'there's no battle here.'
I sit on the floor with him as he struggles with the spaghetti bolognaise, slurping it from his hands into his mouth.
'Nice worms.' Jimmy Waldron never said anything as complimentary about my food. Ever. So there we are, our backs to the couch, sipping Irish Mist that's left over from the divorce party. The heat warms my face and he tells me what happened, the scent of mountain and stream easing from his clothes. He and his men

were out hunting, in pursuit of a particularly fine stag, Bran and Sceolan barking and chasing the prize, way beyond the upper Dodder valley. The day was so fine he didn't know which gladdened his heart more, the birds singing in the glen or the fine antlers of the stag as they gained on it. The triumphant cry as they brought it down echoed throughout the hills. They were heading towards his own mountain, Seefin, when they came upon three beautiful women who offered them food and drink. The sun was at its hottest and they were glad to sit and drink with them, their prize catch ready to bring home, the dogs sleeping off the chase. While he was cutting out the heart of the stag to feed to the dogs, he could hear his men laughing and courting the women. Then they went silent, one by one. He crept back to where they were and what he saw chilled his blood. His men were frozen like statues among the gorse and the heather. He threw the stag's heart at the women and they drew swords on him, screaming as the blood spattered all over them. Then before his eyes all their beauty began to fall away – hair turning grey, skin wrinkling, teeth rotting.

'I know the feeling, exactly,' I say. Full body meltdown. But he doesn't seem to hear me. A high pitched scream was coming from their shrivelled mouths. He knew he wasn't safe from one deranged woman, let alone three. So while they were cleaning the blood out of their eyes, he crawled through the furze and snaked along the ground. He could hear them still screaming while he headed towards an

underground souterrain, a chamber which had an exit to the other side of the mountain. But his whole underworld landscape had changed. Some devilish beast must have come and eaten up the passageways because he couldn't find his normal route. That's how he ended up in the middle of that frightening place. What did I call it?
'The Square. Yea, them property developers; you think this place is bad? Sure they've destroyed the whole country. Devilish is too good a word for them.'
'I need to get back to see what has happened to my men.'
'As soon as it's dark, I'll take you.'
'In your chariot?'
'No, my Ka, but it does the job grand.'
So we sit there in my sitting room, talking. I'm itching to switch on *Sex in the City* but I can't take a chance in case he takes his sword to the telly.
When I see Mary Stephens across the street pulling her curtains on the evening I know we can move. With a bit of difficulty negotiating his sword, I coax him into the passenger seat. Not a sinner takes any notice of us as I drive my little chariot down by the shops, out onto the Old Bawn Road, down by the Mill House and round the roundabout. Finn is hanging onto his seat belt and his sword as I head up towards Bohernabreena. We drive up the snaking roads, take the turn for Glenasmole. Only when he starts to recognise his hunting ground does he relax. When Seefin comes into view I stop the car.
'You're a good woman,' he says as he touches my

cheek. Then he's gone. Pity Jimmy Waldron didn't think so.

I watch him walk into the mountain, see a change come over him; his strength return; his stature increase; then his warrior shadow get darker and darker as he climbs towards the sky. Soon I cannot see him at all. I turn the car and head towards home. As I drive back down the mountain I watch the lights of the city eating up the dark; notice how easily they block out the stars.

Geraldine Mills

Wolves

Once, when this whole island was all forest, a village was troubled by wolves. In those days, wild things lived beneath the trees. Gigantic oaks flowered like cathedrals. Great elk kicked up puffs of pine needles, and stood in the moonlight, basking their antlers. There were bears and dark creatures we've never seen and at times outside the limit of the village, a quietness would fall where just the drip of dew off fern could be heard and fear would clasp your heart.

That winter the wolves howled all night every night it seemed, but were rarely seen. One look and the shadow you thought was shaped like the devil himself was gone like a dream into the dark. Once, the mead house-keeper's daughter, carrying water from the well after midnight, thought she saw a great wolf sat on a doorstep as calm as a dog licking his paw, but by the time she could blink it was gone.

It happened one day that an herb-woman that lived in this village, decided to stray into the forest of a morning and visit her grand-daughter who had fallen sick with fever. She walked the ancient road, the Slighe Mór, that went from the heart of the kingdom from the great hill of Tara to who knew where. She walked into a green-dark silence you can only imagine and felt beneath the trees a terrible coolness, even though the day was fine.

Soon she had reached King John's bridge, a hump of rough stone crossing the stream. She liked to stop there and look over at the little view it gave of what lay ahead. The little bridge marked the beginning of Lord Rokeby's demesne – the land became wilder in the forest around his estate, which was good for hunters, but for no one else. If her grand-daughter had not been seamstress to the lady of the house herself, her family would not have allowed her to take a little cottage on the borders of the grounds. As it was the lady of the house preferred her near to her at all times, for making calf-skin gloves, for stitching travelling cloaks, for making dresses woven out of peacock feathers for masked balls. Her grandmother sighed at the thought of her grand-daughter sewing new riding gloves in the firelight, her eyes blinded by wood-smoke.

She walked on, and the day grew drab and a drizzle came down from the low clouds to make it seem like dusk, and the forest grew colder and less friendly by the moment. Once, a wolf howled and the sound travelled oddly between the trees, so that it was hard to tell whether it came from near or far. She stopped for the moment, thinking of rumours she'd heard by the well-side – tales of men turned to beasts, and beasts turned to men and creatures that were a peculiar mix in-between. Just thinking this in a place such as this was enough to make the bravest man in the village swallow his pride and turn tail, but this herb-woman was the sensible sort and not to be troubled by superstitions and childish fears, and as for old wife's tales, she'd invented most of them herself.

Soon, she had come to the oculus in the wall to Lord Rokeby's demesne and she peeped through the gap to a deep wooded valley with a river passing beneath. The oculus was a grand thing - a carved peep-hole, as wide as a well-head and deep enough to lean two elbows on, if only you had the leisure to gaze. It had fine details in its stonework, the faces of angels and two sea creatures she could not recognise, blowing their cheeks out as though they were the north wind in a map.

The herb-woman tutted to herself. *If only*, she thought, *my grand-daughter wasn't settled just outside the walls. For what was the use in that! If only Lady Catherine with all her fancies and trifles had a thought for the poor child and kept her safe within the walls of her estate. What would be the use of her to anyone if she's gobbled up by wolves, I ask you?* She leant in elbow-deep through the peep-hole to take her ease and saw that a swathe of new houses had grown like mushrooms within the walls. A whole estate of them. All as new as you like and not a word to anyone. 'More cottages mean more tenants,' she said, 'more trouble, I say.'

'More trouble, indeed,' said a gruff voice behind her.

She turned and saw a tall man wearing a green hunting coat, and a tricorn hat decorated with the auburn feathers of a pheasant. He had, she thought, a rakish tilt of the hips. Who was this, she wondered - a hunter or a poacher? Sometimes, it was hard to tell the difference these days.

'You startled me,' she said, taking hold of a little wooden brooch she wore for luck.

'I dare say,' said the man, and she noticed that he

wore whiskers on his chin as bushy and wild as any blacksmith, but that his cuffs were spilling with the lace of gentle folk. 'The guilt of trespassing is liable to make anyone jump.' The herb-woman drew herself up at this. *Trespassing indeed,* she thought, *says he the stranger!*

'I am on my way to visit my grand-daughter,' she said in her grandest voice. 'She happens to live in the gatekeeper's cottage, in service to Lady Catherine herself.'

'Ah, I see,' said the man, shifting the weight of a sack of game he carried over one shoulder. 'The little maid. You should have spoken sooner. She is a good, kind maid, by all accounts.'

'She is,' said the herb-woman, 'but not, I would imagine, to the likes of you.'

'Now, be fair, be kind,' said the man, smiling and showing the red of his mouth and the white of his teeth. 'We are all here in service to Lord and Lady Rokeby, and anything we say or do must be forgiven in light of how we aim to serve, mistaken though it may be. Let me now make full amends for my offence.' He held out his arm, almost daintily. 'Let me introduce myself. I am Charles Le Salle, furrier, hunter and woodsman. Would you let me accompany you to your grand-daughter's cottage?'

'I suppose,' the herb-woman said, thinking it was better not to provoke when it was possible to soothe. She waved away his arm, adding, 'I am too old, mind, for all that nonsense.'

She took the path that continued along the perimeter

of the estate, walking on a little ahead so that she might make good time and avoid the bother of conversation.

'You really needn't take the trouble,' she said, as she walked. 'Walking with me will be hours lost from your day for nothing.' 'It is no trouble at all,' said the man. 'This is where I please to go in any case. And besides, you shouldn't be out in the forest alone close to dark. There are too many wolves, this season. Did you not hear one howl moments before we met?'

'I did,' said the herb-woman, 'but let me tell you from someone longer in this world than most. There are worse things in the world than a wolf.'

He unhitched his hunting knife from his belt. 'Look at this, now,' he said, 'The tools of my trade. I travel through these woods with my axe in one hand and my knife in the other. One for the trees I am commissioned to bring down and the other for any trouble that comes my way. See here, mistress, this knife point has given me three fine wolf pelts this summer, creatures with more teeth and claws than you can guess and I have the scars down my arms to prove it. Do not tell me now that there is a worse thing than a wolf.'

The herb-woman held her tongue this time, but could not help but think his knife and axe rather too much for an afternoon stroll.

They walked on at a steady pace and soon the forest thinned ahead of them, the trees falling away to a clearing of burnt grass.

'What's this now?' exclaimed the herb-woman, 'this

is not the same path as before.'

'The same path and better,' he said, 'safer, too. Think now of the little houses that shall soon be built along this path, and how secure you shall be. And look further in – you'll see that the trees have been thinned out further and further than ever before. And all, I might add, by commission of our good Lord Rokeby.'

'But I would not recognise the place,' said the herb-woman. 'I used to walk this way as a girl, and it was all meadows and wildflowers, and the sound of the trees over everything.'

'You do not come this way much now, I'd guess,' he said.

'When I can - when there's some need.'

'You'll see much change then, more houses than you can count. Lord Rokeby noticed that there was something of a craze for the bath house on his grounds – every sort of pilgrim you could imagine. Come to take the waters and then to stop here after that for the good of their health. You should be happy your grand-daughter has so much company.'

The herb-woman could not help but frown at that. She did not like the bath house much, as it smelt of sulphur, much like Lord Rokeby himself. And she could only imagine how difficult it would be to make a living in a place such as this. It was bad enough for those who had sufficient luck to be settled in the village. Only someone who thought purely of gold would sell poor folk a patch of burnt grass on the edge of nowhere. 'I'm sure,' she said, 'that there are all sorts of company, but not all of it is good.' He stopped on the path. 'I can see that I have foraged up for myself a homespun philosopher the like of which you wouldn't find in court. So, why don't we settle this particular argument with a little wager? Why don't you tramp along this dreary old road the high kings built god knows when, whilst I cut through the fine new estates at a clip so fast I will be sipping wine in your daughter's parlour an hour before you're home.'

'Do as you please,' the herb-woman said, thinking the fine new estates looked more like her little dispensary garden when it got trampled to muck by the brewer's pigs. 'But you won't be drinking wine, for she hasn't a cellar, nor a parlour for that matter.'

He bowed at that, to put an end to any further argument, and without a word turned and strode across the scorched grass. She walked on, not changing her pace, and not worried about any wager – she enjoyed the quiet, stopping occasionally to listen to a wood pigeon, or to pick up some rare flower from the edge of the path.

As she walked on she noticed the lay of the land change more and more, just as the man had promised. Little wattle settlements grew up more and more, in haphazard places, all on top of each other. They seemed flimsy to her. 'Blow away at the first sign of a breeze,' she thought. And yet, someone was expected to live in them someday, at the edge of nowhere, with no village around as protection and no well to draw from. It seemed a strange settlement to her.

After a time, just as the sun was sinking into the earth, she viewed the smoking chimney of her granddaughter's cottage, and felt a shudder inside in anticipation of warming her feet at the hearth.

She walked up through her grand daughter's garden - it was lush with Wild Thyme, Harebells, Restharrow and Traveller's Joy, and countless other flowers and herbs they had planted together. There was a smell of late summer and smoke, of the forest and rain. She noticed the hunter's bag laid out over her granddaughter's wood pile. *Foolish to leave it out*, she thought. *You can't be so careless with meat.* She peeped in – he'd taken more than she could easily count – leverets, pheasant, partridge and even a small fox, though who would eat a fox she couldn't imagine. And there, something new, the bag was laid on a whole wolf pelt – it had the paws on complete. She lifted one and thought it not much worse than a dog.

The chill was coming on so she rapped firmly on the door three times, 'It's only granny, dear,' she said, 'brought you a honey tincture to soften that cough.'

The grand-daughter's voice came weakly through the door, 'Just push on the door, granny and come through – the latch is open.'

The herb-woman did so, thinking, *foolish girl, does she imagine her little house is a palace with footmen at the door?* She stopped where she stood, her arms on her hips. The little kitchen was empty.

'So, where are you, my dear? I can't see you.' She

sniffed the air – she could smell Wild Mint and something else – there was a raw tang in the air.

'Why granny,' a voice said, almost beside her, 'I'm right in front of you and you can't spy me out!'

The herb-woman looked around her, suddenly frightened by something she couldn't name, and then saw a figure in silhouette at the kitchen table.

'I'm taking the vapours from a basin, just like you used to suggest,' the voice said, 'come closer.'

The herb-woman looked hard and saw a bit clearer and sat at the table. 'The light is not good here,' she grumbled, and you must remember that your granny is old and for that matter, your voice sounds deeper than ever despite taking steam. I shall make you some tea in a moment.'

'In a moment, yes. But sit still and rest yourself. My voice may be deep, granny, and all thick with steam, no doubt, but it is all the better to speak with you.'

'I'm sure. So, is her ladyship treating you right? Let me see those beautiful fingers she works to shreds. My, they have grown rough, and my dear, hairy at the knuckles too.'

'Nonsense, granny, to say such a thing.' Her granddaughter shook the cloth off her head and dark hair flowed down to cover her face. 'Now, say I don't look better than ever.'

'I can hardly see you well enough to say anything,' the herb-woman said. 'Light some candles before I go blind trying to look.' She squinted in the bad light. 'My, when you smile your teeth shine out and seem

bigger than ever.' Her grand-daughter leaned forward out of the kitchen shadow and the herb-woman saw the half-wild face of Charles Le Salle.
'Shh,' he said, 'too much noise might wake the dead.'
The herb-woman stood up, the chair scratching back against the wall with a jolt. 'Where's my grand-daughter?' she said, 'Oh mercy, what have you done?
Charles Le Salle's face turned inquisitive like a wolf does when it is trying to understand human speech. 'Nothing that I haven't done a thousand times before, my good woman, whilst hunting in these woods in the name of Lord Rokeby.' He paused, then said in a bored voice, 'Look to the fire place.'
She turned and saw the fire glimmering and letting out the odd spit in the silence. 'You might smell a greasy sort of smell,' he said, 'and even see a shred of hair remaining on the grate.' He stood up, and jumped over the table. 'Lady Catherine has a new dressmaker just recently, I think you'll find. Someone a little more sophisticated. She gets bored of the same country fashions, week after week. And as for the lord, well, he can't keep a mistress forever on his ladyship's doorstep, so he sent me out a-hunting. Shame really, she was a pretty little thing. A bit simple though – would you believe she had a little wolf cub as a pet in her garden? They're not for pets though, I'm sure you realise. Vicious things, in fact. Vermin. I had to slit its throat.'
He stepped forward and she flinched, his hand at her neck, just resting there for the moment. 'There was the house too, of course. Surplus to current

requirements. Lord Rokeby has big plans – plans to sell up for one thing, and all of this part of the forest shall be cut down. Of course, he doesn't want to hang round too long after that happens. 'Damn too uncomfortable,' as our lordship would say. Soon the place will be swimming with pilgrims and industry, folk say. They will set up an Ironworks named after the Phoenix of myth. The drive to the house shall be named Black Avenue. No, my good woman I think you'll find this place near unrecognisable given a year or two. And as for his lordship, well he'll pocket the gold and sail back home, to the other country, like so many have done before him. The Rokebys' can live in the city then and her ladyship can ride to town and wear a new dress every day of the week if she pleases. Won't that be nice and convenient for everyone involved? He'll leave his name behind, of course - you have to give a name to a place, if nothing else. And he'll need agents like myself to collect the rents and keep the inquisitive like your good self in order.'

'Stop twisting now,' he said, his voice suddenly impatient, 'you're worse than a hare caught in a trap. Quiet now. That's better. It's just a swift crack of the neck and it's all over - you don't even have time to think. But you must keep still first.' She shook suddenly in his grasp, and he stood back, his hands clutched to his chest, blood on his hands. 'You bit me me,' he said, his voice outraged. 'Not bit,' she said. 'You left your knife on your bag outside.' He fell back on the floor in front of the hearth, the blood spreading on his silk waist coat like ink on manuscript. 'You've killed me, you witch,' he said, his voice coming in gasps, 'You'll hang for this, you know? They'll find you out.' 'Not me,' she said softly.

She walked out. As she passed through the little garden she flung the bloody knife onto the midden. She walked out through the gate, leaving it open behind her – there was no point worrying anymore about such things.

Soon her breath had calmed. She walked the dark path that led back home through the forest, not seeing the burnt grass and wattle houses as she passed. Soon, the moon came out to light her way and wolves began to howl far and near, but the herb-woman did not notice.

David Mohan

Citti's Cure

As daughter of Lord West's cook, Citti was no stranger to blood. She played in red puddles after battles during her childhood, and saw many a poor boar split open from belly to snout in the kitchen. Somehow she was unprepared for the sight of her own.

It had been a hot dusty day in the newly acquired land, Tasagart, and she took to wading in the cool waters of a shallow lake, when a fierce and demonic looking eel approached. Blacker than the darkest night, he used his many rows of precise pointed teeth to take a chunk, just the size of a cider apple, out of her ankle and made away with it, sniggering as he slithered. Then blood, her blood, gushed forth from the wound, mingling with the lake's waters.

Up to that moment she'd looked helplessly on, at the whole thing. Citti had always been a drowsy, clumsy sort of plain looking specimen, whose highest hope in life was to be allowed stay on in her mother's kitchen, peeling onions and plucking fowl. She hadn't looks nor sense to aspire even to the role of server for banquets, at that moment, however, everything changed.

As Citti's blood flowed, it seemed to take with it all doubts and nerves she had ever felt. A great calm descended upon her and she lifted the injured foot high up above her head, like one of the contortionists at court. This stopped the blood flow and she moved first heel then toe of the other foot in a slow gradual movement until she thus made her way out of the lake. At the edge, she staunched the wound with a dock leaf and ran to her mother's hut near the chief's tent. There,Citti senior was too busy cleaning gizzards for the pot to give her daughter more than a glance, she did notice the child seemed unusually quiet and free of fidgeting compared to her normal self though.

Citti's mother fell back against the side of horse that was strung up on the wall when she did turn to look at her child. The girl was glowing, radiant. The squinty little eyes had been replaced with bronze shining globes and her hair was silvery and shining from within.

'Tell me Citti, have you seen anyone else since this mishap?'

'No ma-am.'

And indeed it was apparent, because the first man to see her was an aging messenger of the chief, who was halted as though his feet had met quicksand when he first beheld the transformed child, and clutched at his heart to stop it from jumping out of his chest to meet her, while his eyes watered from her beauty. Gradually more and more of the staff beheld her, until the whole army and even the chief had heard of this wondrous creature. Her strange beauty was told of throughout the land within weeks.

Her energy was fading, because of the injury. She'd do nothing all day but lie down near her mother's cooking pit, her beautiful features listless. It kept most of this company of the Norman army awake at night worrying about it. They whispered sadly about how magical and wonderful it would be to solve the problem for her. Most of them agreed they would happily have died to do so.

At length, since the problem had been caused in a local waterway, Lord West decided it would be best to consult with a local expert for advice. All fingers pointed toward the cave of Dosacra when such an expert was sought. West himself went to see him, such was his concern for the young lady, whom he now believed might be a suitable Lady for himself, once cured.

Lord West found the old man – alleged to be an indirect descendant of Mosacra the monk, was pouring strange liquids from vial to vial – with smoke billowing from the cups.

'I presume you are working on something for my bride to be?' Lord West asked, for the first time saying out loud what his intentions were. Dosacra chuckled to himself, but didn't allow his intent concentration slip.

'No, this is my lunch, my lord, I will do the girl foot fixer in another moment, shouldn't take too long.'

West watched the old man for awhile. Finally Dosacra stopped and fixed his beady eyes on him.

'So' he said.

'So, yes, the girl foot fixer you called it?'

The old man chuckled again. 'No, that, was my own poor attempt at a joke. The problem will not be easy to fix, I fear.'

'Oh!' West sat down, disconsolate.'Yes, there is a lot of work to be done if we are to help this poor girl.'

'I am willing to do anything.' The old man told him what must be done. The first thing needed was a huge palace, one thousand paces from the cool water lake. It didn't matter that this was only down the way a little from a brand new castle that West had built, the palace had to be erected down near Dosagart's octoganol dwelling and Citti would stay there while awaiting her cure.

A replacement for the chunk stolen from Citti had to be found. A small smooth stone would come from the shores of the lake and Dosacra himself would choose it from a number of possibilities – to be brought to him, one each from each woman in the locality.

Those were the easy bits. The job of actually saving her was complicated and highly skilled. The stone would have to be precisely inserted into the wound, but not by hand. It had to be struck with a silver sword, had to fly fast and high through the air before the final landing being cushioned by a silver albatross – who would arrive at exactly the right time, which was exactly one year on from the initial incident – the summer solstice. The thing was that the person striking the stone had to be standing at least 30 horse lengths from the lady, and must prove their skill beforehand. If the stone was struck and met the wrong target – she could be killed. Thus there would be a great competition to determine who could best control the speed and direction of such a projectile.

Lord West put out a call around the land, and even

to the neighbouring countries – the best shots-man had to be found to handle the task. A practice ground was set up around the grounds of the palace where the beautiful girl was now living. They had trouble finding albatrosses, but a few of the tame eagles about the place were trained to fly among them, and in case they weren't distraction enough – there was a flag with a stick and a wildly flapping rag stuck into each target that they aimed towards. This was something the men normally only saw in battle, so it tested their nerves greatly. It was summer when this began and all local men in the area practiced the challenge faithfully for the remainder of the year, in all weathers, in preparation for the great competition.

Dosacra even joined in, for though he didn't have the same strength as the rest of the men, it was clear the walk and the talk were enjoyable, and led to many of the men becoming firm friends because of the long distances they walked and the adversity they sometimes had to cope with when their stones would go astray. One month before the big competition, word came that a Scottish shepherd, called Colbán Montgom, had been found who could strike the ball true, for – although they had never had a use for it – the Scots had discovered the recreational possibilities of hitting stones into rabbit holes while passing long days on the highlands.

When he arrived the man was shy and unassuming and readily agreed when Lord West told him – 'even if you win the competition and fix the beautiful Citti, I am to marry her when she is all better, and this

palace will forever be associated with our names.'
The shepherd merely shrugged, not in it for women or fame, he'd seen the lass, and though she was glowing and radiant and all the things people said, she was a bit too grand for his tastes. He couldn't have imagined her helping him with gutting a sheep, or coping with the tough skin hardening winds.

The shepherd won the competition easily, and the local townspeople were very admiring and enjoyed watching his skill. He then fixed the girl with one shot, aided as predicted by the wondrous silver Albatross, who then celebrated in the air with all the eagles used in practice as well as many other birdies of the air. Beautiful Citti danced the night away at a fantastic banquet in the arms of handsome Lord West. In the morning they were to have the wedding breakfast. All were gathered, and Lord West eagerly awaited his bride. She arrived, but she was not as he remembered. She had lost all glisten and glow, she walked awkwardly, had squinty eyes, and a dull bored face. Lord West almost asked her what she had done with his Citti, but he saw the glint in Dosacra's eyes, and remembered some stories he'd heard about how she'd been quite dull before the incident. He stood in front of everyone and cleared his throat.

'Good men, we have practiced many a long day to fix this… this…' He looked at her, but out of habit could call her nothing but '…beautiful creature. And it's true I had planned to take her as my wife.' Citti giggled awkwardly at this and scratched at her head. 'But, alas, it cannot be. Citti you belong with your hero Colbán, the man that saved you with his natural talent. Praise and honour to you both.'

The crowd cheered generously, and Citti smiled suddenly her old black toothed smile. Her shepherd hero grasped her then in a manly hug. They went home happily to Scotland.

The men got up the next day and continued with their practicing to save her, as fervently as before, as though they were preparing for another such incident. And they still practice there to this day.

Niamh Bagnell

The Spear of Lugh

Winding halls, shaped from the mists of time, were set down in ethereal forests of silk. Rivers flow through woods filled with trees, lush with emerald leaves. It is here the three goddesses spend their days, it is here they first grew uneasy. Eriu, Banba and Fodla walked restlessly through their kingdom remembering the days when the Spear of Lugh was doused in crushed poppies and placed in Dagda's bottomless cauldron. They were days of much anguish and strife but much feasting and merriment also. Those days were no more the goddesses knew nor did they wish to return to the old ways of steel and strife. Yet, they still craved to weave magic over the landscape of Earth and so, the three of them decided to re-awaken the Spear of Lugh from its drowsy sleep.

The Spear of Lugh slumbered in the giant black cauldron housed in the farthest end of the long halls. How often it had thirsted for blood, to hear the cry of battle, to clash again with enemies such as Balor of the Evil Eye and emerge victorious and sated. Now, it was no longer a threat to life or limb yet Erius, the oldest goddess and after whom Eire was named, spoke her longing to revive its magic but for good instead of evil.

Banba and Fodla agreed but they knew that they would first have to persuade Dagda to change the force fields of destruction. Erius, who was also the most beautiful of the goddesses, with golden hair and tawny coloured eyes, was chosen to first of all beseech the warrior Lugh to relinquish his hold over the spear and then to gain the permission of Dagda to cast the spell of change.

***

Lugh was so smitten by Erius that this first task was only a matter of uttering the words. To Lugh, the voice of Erius was so sweet, so like the scent of heather on the Dublin Mountains he'd walked as a young boy, that he could not refuse. When she spoke he once more felt the soft green moss beneath his feet. Above him a heron opened wings wide to embrace the universe, and all about him was heavy with the fruits of plenty. He assured the goddess, while looking deep into her eyes, that as soon as Dagda cast the spell of change, he would willingly wash the blade clean of all its mischief. Dagda was another matter entirely.

'You know I'm the God of Good,' he told her 'and I want nothing but unlimited bounty for my people. That is why my living harp plays the music of joy for all. When was the last time mourning or grief struck its melancholy chord?'

Erius had to admit that the harp indeed played nothing but solace and comfort, music that brought Sika from their hiding places and pushed the shiniest root and branch through the deepest soil. Dagda told Erius that he was afraid the day might come when his people would once more have to go to battle, to defend honour, to ward off enemies.

Erius was not disheartened. She took the leaves of the blackthorn tree and made a soothing drink for Dagda, one that induced dreaming in the great God. In the dream Dagda saw the spear of Lugh facing upwards towards the sky. Released from its captivity in the cauldron, it torched the evening with a light that caused those who saw it to lift their eyes towards the heavens and give thanks for such a great blessing.

He summoned Erius and gave his blessing. 'Where will you place this treasure?' he asked, looking with new tenderness at the young goddess. 'In Tallaght,' she replied, 'where else but in a place that has opened its heart to peoples of many tribes, many nations?' Dagda gave thanks and was pleased and so it was done. In the middle of Tallaght village, the Spear of Lugh can be seen peeping up from behind Spar Supermarket and across the road from the building which once housed Tallaght Community Arts Centre. The Tallaght Echo newspaper is there also and it seemed to Erius that the Spear fitted into this setting as a sign of peace and hope in times of upheaval.

Eileen Casey

Dead Lives

My great grandfather, Thomas Purcell, wrote about the place where he was born. He was a writer just like me, in the days before the formation of the Northern European Archipelago. Like him I write for those who come after me. He wrote about his country – a concept that has long since ceased to exist – and he wrote about his life. He wrote about the people who lived in the small village he came from, a place called Clondalkin.

The site of this place no longer exists, but if you are lucky enough to acquire a travel permit and take the shuttle west from Terminal Metropolis 3, you will pass close enough to where it used to be. If you remove your Virtual Sense Pads and use your actual eyes to look below you will see only mile after mile of grey water washing against the crossed girders of the elevated rail. Somewhere underneath the tide lies Clondalkin, a modern Atlantis.

The life of that place is as dead as my great grandfather. All of the monuments are gone forever, and the memory of them almost sputtered out. They live on only in his notebooks, in the accounts he wrote of life as it was lived back in the early twenty-first century. He wrote about men and women he knew, about work and play, about churches and school kids and football and hurling matches, things of which I know nothing. He wrote about sunlight reflected on the still water of the canal on bright winter days, about green grass and tall trees, and traffic jams and unemployment. He wrote about the smell of new cut grass mixed with two-stroke petrol on balmy summer days, the noise of car alarms shrieking for attention in the dead of night, the friction from cheap polyester collars scarring the necks of low-paid supermarket workers. He wrote about his wife and children, about visiting friends and eating and drinking together. He wrote about joyful times; the births of babies, weddings and celebrations, and he wrote about sad things also, about suffering, disease, regret and death.

Sometimes when I read his notebooks I wonder how people lived like that, their lives inextricably bound up with so many others, with no space to call their own. Imagine the niggling demands of constant interaction, the emotionally draining encounters of the quotidian, the indignity of such proximate living and dying. So unlike our lives now. I live in West Metropolis 3, one of the ten Metropolises in the Northern European Archipelago. I stay in my rooms almost all the time and travel only when my work demands it and a permit is arranged on my behalf. There are no windows in my rooms – there is nothing to see outside anyway. Fresh air is transmitted through an ingenious arrangement of flexible tubes to each abode. Sunlight also has been replaced by a more consistent and less harsh synthetic light that is powered by the nuclear grid on behalf of the whole of the United States of Europe.

I live alone, but am on a waiting list to be assessed for cohabitation with a like-minded female. My prospects are good I believe. I was well trained as a boy. At school we learned all about our world, what makes it work, and how we can work to make it an even better place. We celebrate who we are quietly in our own abodes on holidays such as World Nuclear Power Day. As children we were taught to be positive, we were warned about the negativity of looking back, and I understand that this is as it should be. But I keep my great grandfather's notebooks nonetheless, even though I know it is a crime. My father taught me how to decipher his gnomic script as his own father taught him. From time to time I sit with the notebooks on my lap – I block out all of the many other distractions that we call information and entertainment – and imagine what his town was like back then. Soon I am there with him in Clondalkin, a living, bustling town, no longer buried beneath the grey swell of noiseless waves.

I transcribe from his notebooks: *History lives here, all around us, in between the terraces on the estates, in the yards behind the shopping precinct in the old village, on the narrow streets where cars are backed up belching fumes, under my booted feet as I walk on in haste to where it is I'm going. Look closely. A ruin idles here, an ancient graveyard slumbers there; beyond that graffitied wall a holy well dries up, and look – a Round Tower rises from the side of the road not fifty yards from the queuing crowds outside the Post Office! History is everywhere here, dead lives whispering to us from all sides. They know nothing we can use, we have no time for them,*

*and so we ignore them vigilantly. We pass them by,
but at what cost?*

Brian Kirk

Hell Fire Club

There are many myths and legends written about the Hell Fire Club. The most vivid story is that the devil was seen there and it is haunted to this day by a big Black Cat with fire in his eyes. It is recorded that it was built by William Connolly the Speaker in the House of Commons in 1729. Before the house was built a large Cairn stood on the summit of Mount Pelier Hill. Connolly is said to have destroyed this when he built his house over it. When the roof was blown off sometime later in a great storm this was attributed to the Devil in revenge for the desecration of the Cairn.

The Hell Fire Club became well known by the gentry who came from all the castles in the Tallaght area, BelgardCastle, Tymon, Drimnagh, Kilnamanagh to name but a few, plus hunting lodges. These people reigned supreme over all of Tallaght and its lands and the Dublin mountains. There was one man in particular who was very popular because of his money and wit and could procure women of ill repute from Dublin City. They were brought by horse and carriages up the steep hills and paths to the Hell Fire Club for the amusement and gratification of the gamblers and drinking lords. Legend has it that to this day hikers and hill walkers on the the steep roads up Kilakee have reported feeling the breath of horses and the eerie laughter of women, the shivering presence of evil. This makes them bless themselves and ask for God's help. It is said because of all the gambling, debauchery and immoral behaviour that went on, the Devil was in his element. But as good will overcome evil, it was discovered that this very rich, slick man was discovered to have cloven feet when a playing card fell to the ground. He was challenged to explain himself. The story goes he turned into a big Black Cat with an arched back, splayed claws, and his eyes were roaring with fire. He scattered the money, drink, playing cards, people dived for cover from his fangs. It is said he went up through the roof in roaring flames bringing the roof with him.

If one stands in Old Bawn, Tallaght today and looks up the Dublin Mountains towards Bohernabreena and Kilakee you can see the Hell Fire club. It is still very visible and attracts many visitors. But be warned if you have a few drinks and feel the need for some excitement, don't try making your way up the steep ancient path. You will only hear groans of evil spirits with pounding hearts, the smell of sweating horses, the presence of evil. Beware the Devil is about and he's out to get you!

On winter nights with the wind howling, screams of horror and despair can be heard over these very mountains that are so beautiful in the summer, but on winter nights like these it is said the Banshee is on the prowl frantically trying to get back into the Hell Fire Club again. She can be seen silhouetted by the moon;

the Big Black Cat with yellow eyes blazing, showing large fangs as he invites her to ride on his back as he rides to hell.

Julie Coombes Kiernan

.

Journey's End

As soon as he returned from Tir na nÓg, misfortune had visited Oisin in the hollow in the Dublin hills that borders the counties of Dublin and Wicklow. Fate decreed that he could never return to Tir na nÓg. A broken man, he was too old and frail to move far from the place of his doom. He spent the remainder of his days being cared for by a servant boy, Gearoid, who was honoured to serve the son of the legendary Irish chieftain, Fionn McCumhaill. Together they rambled amidst the evergreen cypress, yew and fir trees and rested in the shade of the pine groves. Then they made camp and slept by the sparkling water of the River Dodder. As the days turned into months, they grew very close.

Between Seafinn and Ballymorefinn Hill, Oisin sat and remembered the glory days of the Fianna; the hunting, fishing and feasting that he shared with his brave father, Fionn, and his companions as a youth. He had been so happy with his beloved Niamh Cinn Oir, Niamh of the Golden Hair. The three hundred years he had spent with her in Tir na nÓg had only felt like three, to him.

Now his comrades were long dead and gone and he would soon be joining them. Each day his step became slower; his eyes grew dimmer, until alas, he could not see any of nature's beauty around him. Guided by the faithful Gearoid, he breathed in the clean air, ate fish fresh from the lakes and recounted tales of an Ireland now long gone.

One evening, as the long summer was coming to a close, as he lay resting in the lush green grass, his eyes were opened and suddenly, he could see again. Enraptured, he watched the sun turn the sky into gold, as golden as his beloved Niamh's hair. He remembered how she had stolen his heart the instant they met and lured him away on her magical horse. Far away from his kinsmen, to Tir na nOg.

They had been blissfully happy there in that timeless land, but he had missed his Irish homeland. His thoughts returned again and again to his father, Fionn McCumhaill and the Fianna.

He'd longed to return to Erin for just a fleeting visit. His beautiful queen, Niamh Cinn Oir, had misgivings about his safe passage on such a long and treacherous journey. She'd told him his feet could never touch Irish soil, or he could never return to Tir na nOg.

She had given him her beautiful white horse that had magical powers, to take him over the oceans and back again in safety. He'd vowed that he would not dismount from the horse on Irish soil. Seeing the lush green pastures of Erin and chatting to his countrymen would be more than enough for him. Then he'd return and they would be together forever in the Land of Youth.

When his trusty steed had got him to his native land, he'd been shocked to see how puny the Irishmen had become in his absence. A group of them were struggling to lift a great boulder. A giant of a man, he could have moved it easily with one hand. He'd pitied the weaklings and his generous spirit compelled him to go to their aid. With his mighty strength, he'd leant down from his horse, put his hand under the stone and raised it up. But his saddle had broken under the strain and he'd fallen to the ground. Instantly, he'd become this very old man. His eyes had dimmed with age, his great strength had ebbed away and he was very frail. There had been no going back to Tir na nÓg.

Now, as Oisin lay there in the dying of the day, his aching limbs longed for the comfort of his beloved Niamh's gentle embrace. He yearned to see her beautiful face, take her in his arms, kiss her lips and run his fingers through her long golden hair. How happy they had been for three hundred years in the Land of Eternal Youth. How he regretted ever parting from her. Tears came to his eyes when he thought how they had planned to spend eternity together.

In the radiance of the sunset, he struggled to sit up on his elbows to watch the wondrous sky. But a great weariness overcame him and he fell back. Noting his erratic breathing, Gearoid hastened to find a sheepskin and placed it gently beneath his head. Suddenly there was a strange sound; a great flapping of wings overhead. The whole sky was filled with a myriad of thrushes. Scrambling joyfully, they soared, swooped and dipped in never-ending circles. Their sweet song had a strange half-human, half-birdlike tune. It mesmerised the old man and he began to feel drowsy. As his eyes closed for the last time, Oisin's gaunt face became alight with ecstasy. He sensed that his beloved Niamh Cinn Oir was waiting for him. In the golden glow, he realised it was she who had sent the thrushes to carry his spirit back to her in Tir na nÓg. They would be united forever in the Land of Eternal Youth after all.

From that day on, the fertile hollow in the Dublin hills that borders the counties of Dublin and Wicklow was known as Gleann na Smol, Thrushes' Glen. It is a favourite haunt of modern-day walkers and nature lovers who take the road from Old Bawn in Tallaght. They can still hear the thrushes' sweet song emanating from homes they have built in the evergreen branches of cypress, pine and yew, in what is now the beautiful valley of Glenasmole.

Marie Gahan

Killinardan*

The thing that nobody knows is that Tallaght was an important suburb of Viking Dublin. The passes to the south included the coastal road, through Bray and suchlike: but the really warlike Wicklow people, the true savages that could pull your heart out through your nose – they all came down the gap that we know now as the Blessington Road – and Tallaght was the first Viking village they would come to, when they had drunk enough poteen to get wild thoughts about women.

Now, what we have to remember is that when Viking Dublin was up and running, people always think of horny caps and wooden boats and screaming marauders, but it wasn't like that at all. These Scandinavians were the closest thing most wild Irish had seen to some kind of aristocracy that it didn't matter a damn that they weren't really privy to most of the mysteries of the bath and the toilet – they were *cool*, damn it. But, most of all, they weren't Christian. Not a man-jack of them. Not one. At least, not until they started getting married into the local society, and became more Oirish than the Oirish, et cetera. But that's a different story. Our Vikings were the proto-globalists of the early Middle Ages: their boats went everywhere, bringing back the things that delighted everyone, most of all the wild Irish: amber, furs, wine … they hadn't invented cornflakes back then.

Our story has to do with the fact that the soldiers stationed on the Tallaght frontier to keep out the

Wicklow savages were usually the ones who had screwed up badly enough not to tend chickens or go on longboat voyages: probably the undereducated, half-Irish offspring of the Irish-born Vikings. People who sort of knew how things went, but hadn't the cop-on or the strings to get them assignment as Viking warriors to some other more profitable or salubrious posting.

It's well known among the *cognoscenti* that the Hellfire Club was in imitation of local folklore about some building, some structure or other, that had existed at an earlier time. Well, look no further, search no more: *Cill an Ardain,* the Irish phrase, literally means 'the church in the high place' – this was the local refectory, boozer, village centre, and spiritual home of all those half-Irish pagans who used to staff the local fort. What people don't realise is that, while the church is the centre and home of village life among Christians, its pagan version was always located on the distant periphery of Viking settlements – because they'd get up to things late into the night, disruptive things, noisy and full of barking and barfing noises, whoops and hollers and all sorts of interesting bits, the likes of which were never seen again until the onset of the internet, millennia later. Enough of that!

And when the new English *suzerains* came to take stock of their domain, centuries later, their first recordings of places and names in the Dublin Pale included the unlikely name *Cill an Ardain*. So far as linguists know, there was never a 'church in a high place.' Churches were always built either on the site of local holy spots, that existed in Irish folklore before the intrusion of Christianity, or on places more salubriously accommodating to local people and their pieties.

But this particular place was never distinguished by ruined stones or Christian graveyards ... so, what gives? Truth to tell, it was the Viking equivalent of the disco: a place where off-duty half-Viking guards could let down their hair, as it were, kick back, and enjoy the fruits of day-to-day life: young local girls with a vision of themselves as The Viking Queen of Dublin, the proper enjoyment of the newly-discovered fruit of the barley – the distillation of any excess of the local foodstuff into some kind of potable ... and the first-ever local building where the clashing of swords on shields would produce not blood, but blood-frenzy, as the local women would get down to disco-dancing with the young stalwarts of the local defense force. And what was it called in the local vernacular? *Cill an Ardain* – 'the cool place up the hill'. End of story!

Tom Myp

Author's Note: The transliteration of Irish placenames into English is not set in concrete. The word 'ardan', to my knowledge, is a real word and means 'high place' in Irish.

Lord Ballyowen's Legacy

There was a time when all the green and beautiful land west of the city was ruled by a vain and capricious Lord. Only interested in his wealth – all accumulated through the toil of his many poor serfs – this man, Lord Ballyowen, brooded often on his unlucky state. For he was a Lord without a castle. Though the land was bountiful, and his people were able to pay the rents he demanded, there were no gems, nor gold, nor marble for him to plunder. He had no materials from his domain to build a grand enough monument to his greatness.

He spent a lifetime searching for the solution to his deprived condition. As he walked his realm, summarily ordering the imprisoning of one of his people, or the confiscation of a fine bull, or the reaping of a diligent tenant's bountiful field for his kitchen alone, he felt inadequate as he had no spectacular palace to return to. In his unhappiness, he decreed that all his people would too be unhappy. There would be no singing, no dancing, no frivolity nor fancy while he was without his proper fortress.

But, when he reached the age of five decades and five, as he counted his riches, he was struck by a brilliant plan. He was a rich man. While his people were hungry, and by his decrees miserable, his land was fertile and rich. He had trebled the wealth his father had left him. He rattled his coins from one hand to the next as a smile, the first for many years, crossed his face. He called his chief servant to him.'Bring me the best architect in the land. Send my fastest horse for him. I know now how I am going to build my palace, and I am anxious to begin!'

A good servant, he did as he was bid, and within the span of one week's passage, he had found and brought to his Lord the finest architect that lived in the entirety of Ireland. Rochfort was the name of the man, and he came, intrigued by the challenge to build a castle for this great nobleman.

He came before him, in his modest home, that did no justice to his riches and position. Rochfort was bold.

'Lord Ballyowen – how am I to build your palace for you? Your land has no marble for construction. No diamonds or rubies for decoration. No gold for the door handles. No silver for the banisters. What am I to do?'

Lord Ballyowen laughed.

'A problem, my learned man, that has stumped the finest, most brilliant minds. But I have finally worked it out! I have a solution.'

'I am so interested to hear it, sire.' said Rochfort, intrigued.

The Lord put his hand in his pocket and took out some coins. He took one and flicked it, high into the air, with his thumb.

'Do you want me to buy the materials, bring them here?'

'No,' said Ballyowen. 'No, the materials must be from my lands, or I will have no respect. It has to be a symbol of my success. What I am talking about are these.' He clapped his hands, and his chief servant came forward, two bags in his hands. Ballyowen opened the bags and spread their contents out, over his table. They were filled with pennies. Hundreds of pennies. Rochfort was confused.

'I want you to build my palace out of my money!' Ballyowen proclaimed, delighted at his brilliance. 'I will have all my wealth turned into these, the smallest coin, so that you will have the most amount of bricks, and can build me the biggest castle. I want a palace as high and wide as a mountain!'

'A mountain made of pennies?' Rochfort murmured under his breath. He shook his head and pondered.

'I don't know if it can be done..' he began. But the thunderous look on Lord Ballyowen's face stopped him. He realised that this was not a man who would be stopped. He realised that he might never leave this land if he did not fulfill the man's wishes.

'I don't know if it can be done,' he began again, 'but I will not stop until I find a way.'

The Lord was placated and was happy once more.

And so Rochfort began his greatest construction. The men of Ballyowen's land were taken from the fields and given to Rochfort to build the palace. They were unhappy, worried for the families left on the land. Women and children had to take to the farms, in the hope they would not starve. Ballyowen made no allowances – the same amount of rent would be due to him, even as his palace was being constructed. It was a desperate time in the land that was west of the city. Rochfort gathered the men all around.

'He wants a palace as high and wide as a mountain,' he told them.

'And what are we to build it from?' asked the men. 'We have no marble, no gold, no silver. We toil on rich farmlands that make our master rich, but there is nothing in the earth other than the life-giving dirt. There is nothing to build his mountain with.'

'With these we will build it!' proclaimed Rochfort, scattering coins across the ground.

'Pennies?' the men exclaimed, watching the little glittering discs spin and roll. Many were puzzled and shook their heads.

'We will build Lord Ballyowen's palace, as high and wide as a mountain, using only his money – his wealth.'

'A Penny Mountain!' one man shouted out, and they all laughed.

Rochfort shook his head, knowing they would not be so brave as to laugh at their master if he were here. He sent them to start on the foundations: many teams to dig, and haul, and lay the beginnings of this wondrous edifice. He turned to pick up the coins he had thrown, and saw that they were gone. He realised the poor starving tenants had made off with those meagre spoils.

Thus began the construction of the Penny Mountain, as the men all called it among themselves. First a magnificent antechamber, as high as six men. And corridors that wound and wove for miles. Three ballrooms, four libraries, five diningrooms, countless bedrooms, the palace grew. And every floor, wall and ceiling was built using coins. 'It is truly worthy of me,' said Lord Ballyowen when he came to inspect it. The glitter of the coins shone and reflected from his eyes. His vision was transformed in front of him, a place worthy of him. Truly awesome, now the world would know his worth. He barely noticed the men working about him, raising his mountain of wealth from the ground. He was immune to their looks of hatred and hunger.

After many months of difficult work, and separation from their families, the castle was finished. Even the men, forced to construct this towering monument to their subjugation, were in awe. Lord Ballyowen swept in, ecstatic that his palace was finally finished. Rochfort took him from room to room, from ballroom to library to diningroom to bedroom, each as glittering as the last. Their feet pinged as they walked, they squinted where the sun shone and reflected off the metal.

Rochfort took him to the highest room, and out onto the penny balcony, to survey his domain. 'I am pleased,' he said.

'Have we built you your mountain?' asked Rochfort. He waited quietly behind Lord Ballyowen.

'You have,' he answered. 'You may go now.'

'I will go now, my Lord, but may I first be paid?'

'Paid?' asked Lord Ballyowen, disgusted. 'But I cannot pay you Rochfort, all my money is here, in the walls, in the ceilings. All around us.' 'But I must be paid,' he said.

Lord Ballyowen nodded to his servants, who advanced on Rochfort and without warning tossed him from this highest balcony. His body fell for five minutes, so high was the pinnacle of Ballyowen's penny mountain. And when finally he hit the ground, Lord Ballyowen and his servants felt the vibrations of the impact.

'That is odd,' thought Ballyowen as he steadied himself. 'I would not have thought I would feel the judder of his death from up here.' But he gave it no more thought and made his way back inside, and down the many, many, many stairs.

But as he descended he felt another quiver. It started slowly, but the tinkle of destruction gathered a tidal momentum as a bewildered Ballyowen looked about his teetering mansion.

'What is happening?' he cried as the stair beneath him started to crumble and the walls shook. If the good Rochfort had been with him, he might have spotted the sticks, and pebbles, and scraps of cloth dotted among the slipping coins. He would have understood that the poor oppressed workers had not been able to resist taking a few coins here and there and replacing them with whatever bits and pieces they had to hand. And if each of the labourers had only taken a few coins each, it still was enough to weaken the building fatally.

A cacophanous cascade of disintegration, it came crashing down, taking Ballyowen with it, burying him underneath what little of his wealth was left. And his people, with tummies not quite so empty, and clothes not quite so threadbare, gathered round to look at what was left of his mountainous folly. And someone suggested they dance and laugh and sing. For in his lifetime, Ballyowen had forbidden them from being happy, he had forbidden them from dancing and singing and frivolity and fancy. They delightedly decreed that forever onwards, this place would be a place of happiness, of friends and equals where the good things of life would be celebrated.

Standing astride all that was left of Ballyowen's legacy, a man looked around, rueful. 'Not so much a high and wide Penny Mountain anymore.'
'No,' another replied laughing. 'It is more a little Penny Hill.'

Triona Walsh

The Celtic Cat

Among the many stories told of the Emerald Isle of Ireland is the tale of how her great wealth came about and how she blossomed to become one of the richest countries in Europe.

Legend has it that it all started - and ended – at the Mound which can be found close to Kingswood Castle. The castle was built in 1622 by Sir William Parsons but a ruin is all that has remained here since it was set alight by the Irish Army some twenty-four years later.

It was here that Niamh, daughter of Fionn O' Shaughnessy was to be betrothed to Shay, son of Liam O'Murthu. Fionn a fine and fair nobleman of some wealth, had wanted to surprise his daughter whom he loved dearly. He had sent his men to scour the countryside with orders to find the most beautiful place in the land for her marriage to her childhood sweetheart Shay. His men searched for many months and eventually they came back to him with news of the ruins of Kingswood Castle. With the wedding due to take place in October he had two months to ensure everything was in order.

Fionn, on seeing the ruins of the castle himself, thought the location perfect. He employed the most skilled tradesmen and paid them well to repair the damaged castle but warned them not to lose the charm of the ruin where jasmine and honeysuckle were entwined through the bricks and crept up and around the building. As he sat on one of the broken walls, the scent wafting on the balmy air brought back memories of his beautiful wife Roisin and he could feel the familiar pain coursing through him. If only she had survived the birth of their son Ruairi so that she too could enjoy their daughter's wedding. Niamh, only two at the time, hadn't understood why her mother had died and why her baby brother had survived only a few minutes in our world before passing on to the next. He hadn't understood why himself.

The sound of a dog barking pulled Fionn from his reverie and he followed the sound of his Irish Wolfhound Cian. He came to a dense patch of forest, enhanced by the flora and fauna; green, lush grasses, hawthorn and beech trees and blackberry bushes which all encircled this area as if trying to hide the Mound at its centre from the outside world. Cian barked again. No amount of calling and coaxing from Fionn would get Cian to come out and so Fionn used his sword to cut through the heavy shrubbery to get to him. The sickly sweet smell of iron assaulted his nostrils. He was scratched and bleeding, cursing under his breath, by the time he found his faithful dog. Cian was circling a mound where a beautiful slender woman sat washing her clothes in a large basin as the sun's rays shimmered on her long, red, wavy hair. She looked up with eyes as green as emeralds as Fionn stood transfixed, as still as a statue, forgetting how to breathe. He felt as if she could see into his very soul. The moment was broken when

Cian barked again.

He turned to the dog to chastise him and when he looked back the beautiful woman had disappeared. In her place a large black crow perched atop the washboard. It was then that he noticed that the water was red and the clothes piled beside the basin were tunics – covered in muck - and blood! Fionn had heard the stories of Morrigan, one of the Tuatha de Danann *(people of Danu)*, whose appearance as either the lady washing the blood of battle from her laundry or a hooded carrion crow was thought to be a premonition of doom – of your own death or the death of a loved one . . .

'No, please, my daughter is to be wed. Please don't take her life or mine before then,' shouted Fionn. The crow watched him with black beady eyes, its head cocked to one side.

'I'll do anything, anything at all,' he said.

There was a rustle in the undergrowth. Fionn turned but there was nothing there. The forest was deathly quiet as if every animal was waiting, watching. The sun had disappeared and the sky which had been an azure blue was now pure black. My time has come, thought Fionn, I am to die here and Niamh will have no father to walk her down the aisle. No mother and no father at her wedding. Resigned to his fate he called Cian to heel.

But Morrigan, despite her reputation, was not totally evil. It was said that she had often aided warriors if she felt they were pure of heart or if she agreed with their battle and motives. She would use her power and magic to protect and empower them with great strength. She was also known as a Goddess of Fertility and many worshipped her, knowing that although she could bring death it would be an honorable death and death was necessary for rebirth - much like the natural cycle of winter to spring. And so, in her own way, she also brought life – not just never-ending death.

Morrigan, realizing that fate had already dealt Fionn a cruel blow with the death of his wife and son decided to make a bargain with him. As long as he kept his promise she would do what she could to spare his daughter's impending death. Fionn listened to her proposal and with shoulders drooped and a heavy heart he eventually agreed.

 October came and everything was ready for this big event. The town had never seen the like before. Beautiful flowers, iris, sweet pea and pink carnations adorned the arch erected in front of the castle. A huge sycamore tree stood watch, its branches blowing gently in the light breeze. Cooks turned suckling pigs on huge rotisseries while servants chased away dogs who sat, sniffing the air, their mouths salivating as they watched juices spit into the fire sending sparks into the air. Dressmakers, with fingers worked to the bone, put the finishing touches to the colourful gowns and tunics they had made.

But on the morning of the wedding Niamh came down with a fever. The wedding was postponed – eventually to be cancelled. Instead, three days later, Niamh succumbed to her illness and now instead of her wedding her funeral would take place. Everyone, except Fionn it seemed, was heartbroken. When the time came, Fionn knelt beside Niamh – pushed her auburn hair back from her face and kissed her forehead. Her eyes flew open and for one brief moment he thought . . . But no, the gold coins which had been resting on her eyes had slipped as he bent over her lifeless body. He looked into them one final time, beautiful flint blue now a milky white and with the help of her betrothed Shay laid Niamh's body upon a throne bed and carried her to the Mound, close to Kingswood Castle, where Fionn had previously come upon Morrigan. There among the scented flowers, they built a spire beneath her. The priest who was to have celebrated her wedding wiped tears from his eyes as he uttered a final blessing. Fionn then lit a

taper and set the spire alight. As the tinder crackled he spoke quietly to Shay who appeared to gain comfort from his words. The wake went on until glowing embers were all that remained in the dark night. Everyone departed, with the exception of Fionn and Shay who set up camp at the base of the mound and with grief in their hearts eventually fell asleep. The next morning, as a beam of light pierced his eyelids, Fionn woke to see Morrigan standing atop the Mound. He made his way towards her.

She took his hand and brought him to the spire where his daughter had been, and there, nestled at the base of the old hawthorn tree was a beautiful tabby cat with three tiny kittens; two black and one, a tabby with colours of amber and green. Morrigan lifted the kitten gently and placed it in Fionn's huge hands.

'I know that this world has not been the kindest to you,' she said. 'But I had no control over Niamh's death, her cards had been dealt. But, I swear to you that Niamh's spirit is within this kitten and if all who loved her keep their promise to feed and protect her then she will look after this entire Emerald Isle and ensure that prosperity and wealth, as never known before, will be theirs. The keepers and their family will never die from fever or accident but will instead live a long and happy life, dying, only when it is truly their time, in their sleep.'

Fionn smiled and caressed the tiny kitten as it purred contentedly. 'I have spoken to Shay and told him of my pledge,' said Fionn. He will take care of this cat as if it were his true wife Niamh but will in time marry another and bear children who will do the same. Morrigan kept her promise.

The land prospered as never before. Other countries looked to the Emerald Isle to see how they had made this happen and tried to follow suit but none could ever reach Ireland's heights. Time went on. Fionn and eventually Shay, passed to the next world at ripe ages and, as promised by Morrigan, in their sleep. Shay's children and grand-children and great-grand-children continued the tradition and fed and nurtured the beautiful, sleek tabby cat who lived on the Mound. Ireland developed; automobiles, buses, airplanes, vast buildings, a spire in the centre of O' Connell Street and a Luas *(similar to a tram),* one of which would pass by Kingswood Castle and The Mound. Although the Luas was a great asset in connecting Dublin it was to play its part in changing the history of Ireland forever.

It was in October 2009 when Shay *(*nicknamed *The Given),* a direct descendent of Shay O'Murthu, was playing football with his friends. They were playing on a hill; separated from the Mound he visited daily by the sweeping Luas tracks, when he was distracted by the thundering sound of a jets engine. Shielding his eyes from the sparkling sunlight he looked up to see an Air France plane flying low in the sky.
'Watch out,' shouted Damian as he kicked the ball towards him.

With his eyes still dazzled from the sun Shay put his hands in the air to catch the ball but it slipped from his fingers. Not seeing the Luas as it careened around the corner he followed the ball across the tracks as the Luas tried to screech to a halt. Faces looking out from the carriages were frozen in shock, when out of nowhere a huge, sleek, tiger pushed Shay aside.

The Luas eventually halted. The driver climbed from his cabin as Shay sat up dazed and shaken. His friends surrounded him; Damian, Robbie and Niall all looking pale and shocked. Shay stood up and walked to the front of the Luas where a crowd had formed.
'It's only a tabby cat' a voice said.
'It was a huge tiger that I saw, sure it pushed him out of the way,' said another voice. With tears streaming down his face he knelt beside the cat. It opened its eyes weakly – one blue and one green – and took one

final breath. Shay was the only one who knew what the death of this cat truly meant; Morrigan's spell was broken and so too were the hopes and dreams of his fellow countrymen of this Emerald Isle – it truly was the death of the Celtic Tiger . . .

Susan Condon

Ares, Greek God of War

Ares was born the only son of the mighty Zeus and his wife Hera. Ares was known by many different names, 'Leader of Man,' 'Ares of the Mighty Heart,' 'Lord of the Dance,' and by the Romans he was called 'Mars.' He was a handsome man with a long beard that women found attractive.

Ares was disliked by his father Zeus, because he took no part in the conception. There are many myths that say he was born as the result of an immaculate conception. Zeus never had much time for Ares as he didn't feel that he was his real father. When Ares was young he went missing for a few years. Zeus didn't try very hard to find him. Apparently, he was abducted by the Aloadai twins. He was held captive in the bronze jar, where he almost lost his mind. Until the step-mother released him and gave him back to Zeus's assistant Hermes. Hera decided he would be better off going to live with Priapus who trained him in the art of dance and martial arts.

Ares had a half-sister Athena, the Goddess of War. She was an arch enemy of his and was also Zeus's favourite child. Ares lost many battles to her. It was once said that Ares charged at Athena whereby she calmly picked up a rock and smashed it over his head. A bit like my own sisters who wouldn't think twice about smacking me over the head if I tried to use the bathroom before them on a Saturday night.

Ares's war consisted of hand to hand combat and bloodlust. In comparison, Athena preferred war at a distance. She was cold and calculating. This was favoured by the majority of Greeks. Ares was seen as a mercenary, who would fight for either side just to have a chance.

Ares was well known for his love for women and having affairs of the heart. It is said that he had over twenty lovers that bore children for him. His best known affair was with Aphrodite, the Goddess of Romance and Beauty. How did he find the time to fight all these wars, on top of being associated with all these women?

One thing that remains a puzzle is why Ares went to war against his two sons, Phobos, meaning fear, and Daiemos, meaning panic. What madman would go to war with anyone called fear and panic? I can just imagine him going into battle. When he called out for Phobos the fear began to set into his troops. Then to call for Daiemos! Imagine, all that panic setting in! Surely some of his troops must have begun to run away. It's no wonder he lost so many battles.

Martin Shannon

Red Sky

The sun splashed its morning glory across the canvas of the dawn sky. A spectrum of colour comprising red, orange, yellow and everything in between dappled the high level clouds, creating the image of a stairway stretching from the sunrise on the eastern horizon upwards to the very heavens above. As she gazed at this spectacle in wonder, Suzanne could not keep from her mind the simple rhyme "Red sky in the morning – shepherd take warning."

The electricity was still out. In fact, early news reports indicated another two generating stations had failed. But it was fears of her impending redundancy and precarious financial position that had kept Suzanne awake all night. After much twisting and turning, she had finally deserted her bed with the intention of getting some early morning air.

Thus it was that shortly after sunrise, Suzanne found herself approaching the derelict hunting lodge. Known as the Hellfire Club, it sat like some concrete carbuncle upon the summit of Mount Pelier. Suzanne did not give much substance to its mythical reputation as being associated with Satanism and the Occult. Like so many, she simply enjoyed the 20 minute walk to the summit to take in the breathtaking vista of Dublin city and bay.

Suddenly, she was greeted with the unexpected sight of a man standing just in front of the old building. Arms outstretched, he was reminiscent of Leonardo da Vinci's Vitruvian Man. His illuminated body was bathed in astral fire, with light and colours complimenting the sky above. At over six and half feet tall, he was naked from the waist up, wearing only breeches and sandals. He reminded Suzanne of Arnold Schwarzenegger in that old movie Conan the Barbarian.

'Ah Pandora, I saw you approach.' The man spoke with no trace of any accent.

'My name is Suzanne,' she replied.

'But of course it is,' said the man.

'Who are you?' Even though Suzanne felt she should be terrified, his presence had a very calming effect over her. She noticed that Beauty, her small cocker spaniel, seemed completely ignorant of the intruder as she continued to wander about the hilltop.

'I am Prometheus, son of Iapetus. I am the giver of fire and imagination. This has been my home here on Earth.'

'The Hell Fire Club?'

'Yes, its name may have been corrupted by your Christianity, but it was here that at great personal cost, I passed to man the gift of fire, the gift of imagination, of problem solving. With these gifts you have thrived and built your civilisation from nothing. Here you once built a temple in my honour, which later became one of your Neolithic Passage Tombs, before it too was destroyed to make way for that monstrosity behind us,' Prometheus informed her, indicating his displeasure in the direction of the Hellfire Club.

'What do you want?' asked Suzanne. Without responding, Prometheus extended his right forefinger, placing it gently on the centre of Suzanne's forehead. His astral fire now extended itself to surround Suzanne and then she became aware.

Suddenly, she knew of the gods' displeasure with Man and their impatience with his unforgivable refusal to take heed of Mother Nature's warnings against his selfish abuse of the Earth. She knew too that the Earth would eventually die if Man continued unchecked and that for this reason Zeus had decided that enough chances had been granted.

Prometheus had been sent to take back the gift of fire and imagination from Man. The power failures were only the start. No longer would Man be able to repair his technology. Its loss would bring about the end of mankind's civilisation.

'But what do you expect of me?' asked Suzanne.

'I have always been Man's friend and wondered that perhaps you might see an alternative to the inevitable destruction of Man. You are of Pandora, sent by Zeus to destroy man. Who better then to now save him?'

For a time, Suzanne gazed out upon Dublin city pondering upon what she had learned. As the day brightened, she could feel the weak warmth of the sun upon her face and as a simple daisy will reveal itself to the sun, what appeared to be a simple solution slowly presented itself to her.

'Prometheus, you have favoured us in the past with your gifts. Would it be possible for you to do so again?'

'What more would you have me do?' he asked.

'Perhaps you might consider enhancing your gift of imagination to allow us to develop new cleaner technology which can save the Earth and ourselves.'

Contemplating what she had said, Prometheus withdrew the astral fire from Suzanne. 'Your suggestion requires some careful consideration Pandora. In the meantime, I shall allow the repair of your generating stations.'

Then he was gone and Suzanne stood alone on top of Mount Pelier. The spectacle of the sunrise had also passed. Nothing remained to suggest that Prometheus had ever been there. Beauty still wandered over the hillside investigating every scent, offering no witness that anything out of the ordinary had occurred. Suzanne returned her gaze over Dublin and began to wonder whether her meeting with Prometheus had actually taken place at all or perhaps her lack of sleep had finally caught up.

Victoria Mullen

River of Death

The battles raged daily at the place of the strawberry gathering. The men of Sath would range on one bank of the river while those of Noth stood on the opposite side. Battle was conducted mainly with spear but also with bow and arrow. Lukana, commander of the Sathans, was the most skilled spearsman. With his incredible strength and accuracy he accounted for many brave warriors of Noth, penetrating their shields as though mere canopy. His prowess was rivalled only by Cassnoc, commander of the enemy across the water.

Over time the river assumed the name of Death, as it transported fallen men from both armies to the unknown regions downstream.

Lukana grew weary of the conflict. Arriving at his camp one night, he was told that his father, Temploc, might breathe his last before dawn. He knelt by his father's bedside and spoke of his love and his respect. Then he sought Temploc's advice. 'Father, this war has endured for five snow seasons. For six completed new moons now I have questioned its wisdom. Say it now and I shall command my men cast away their arms.'

'My son,' Temploc replied, the voice that once boomed, now a whisper. 'For as long as the strongest spearsman can find his range across the River of Death, the fight should continue.' Lukana nodded and the two men spoke no more.

Earthly life left Temploc's body as dark embraced

dawn. Lukana wept, but silently, for a commander's men must know nothing of his weakness. He washed his face, steeled himself and stepped from his father's tent. Ranged outside, in circles that grew larger, like the ripples in a pond from a stone, stood the brave Sathans, each bearing a flaming torch. When he nodded wordlessly, those closest to him extinguished their torches in Father Earth, followed by those behind them and those behind them again, so that the light disappeared in a rolling wave.

'Men of Sath,' he bellowed. But he could say no more, for at that moment there arose from Father Earth a ponderous boom that tortured the ears with its strength, accompanied by a terrifying movement underfoot. Father Earth shook and rocked, knocking every man to the ground. The movement endured for the time of three arrow-flights.

The warriors of Sath climbed nervously back to their feet, dusted off their war garments and formed themselves once again into their ranks. They looked as one to Lukana for reassurance. He, as is the plight of the commander, had no one to look to but himself. Lukana prayed that when he spoke, his voice would betray no fear.

'Men of Sath,' he proclaimed, his voice as strong as the thunderous roar just gone, 'my father is now on his journey to the seven trials of life. He has issued us a sign that we must continue our war against the Nothans until we are victorious. Let us go now to the River of Death and, in his honour, fight the enemy. Tonight we will cremate his body and celebrate his soul.'

The legions of Sath marched with him towards the place of battle, but none, least of all Lukana, was prepared for the sight that awaited them as they cleared the last of the Great Oaks. For there, where the river should be, lit by Mother Sun, stood a mighty gorge. The ground dropped away to the height of three, perhaps four hundred men. In the valley below snaked the River of Death. And across the ravine stood another mighty valley wall, topped by the men of Noth.

Though the enemy was at twice the accustomed distance, Lukana could clearly see Cassnoc standing before his warriors. He needed no further invitation. Lukana drew back his spear and, with the strength of his every sinew, launched it towards his nemesis. The missile hurtled through the air but fell hopelessly short of its target, dropping instead into the valley and plunging headlong into the water below.

Then he recalled the final words of his father: 'For as long as the strongest spearsman can find his range across the River of Death, the fight should continue.' Lukana realised that Temploc's words had not been a call to continue the conflict but rather been a call to end it. He bowed his head and gave the signal to his spearsmen.

His brothers in arms looked awkwardly at one another, uttering no words. Tallor was first to launch his spear into the valley followed by Noclan. With that, the Sathan spearsmen ranged along the cliff-top, let fly their weapons. For some moments, the missiles filled the sky, like geese departing in advance of the snows, before pelting the water below like so many droplets of rain.

The men of Sath waited for the response of their Nothan counterparts. For some time none came. Then a spear was launched from the hand of Cassnoc. With little delay, the Nothan spears graced the sky, mirroring the return of the geese, before piercing the river's skin.

Lukana decreed to his men before they returned to their families and their farms that the river should henceforth be known as the River of Life.

***

A man and his son sit, fishing on the bank of the river. Overhead they can hear the hum of traffic on the bridge over Liffey Valley. When he reads the sign, Luke has a question for his father.

'Dad, it says 'Abhainn na Life'. Does that mean the river of life?'

'No son. It just means the Liffey.'

'Oh, okay,' Luke replies. He feels a tug on the line. 'Hold on Dad, I've got something.'

His quarry, though heavy does not struggle. When he reels it in fully he sees, to his disappointment, it is nothing more than a stick. It is long and straight, like the handle of a sweeping brush, but thicker and longer, and it is pointed at one end. 'You've got one of those sticks,' his father says. 'I snagged one before right here in this spot.' He takes it from the hook, cleans it with a cloth and hands it to his son. 'Want to throw it back in? Pretend you're in the Olympics?'

The boy needs no further invitation. He holds the stick at its centre, draws it back and lets fly. It merges with Mother Sun before re-entering the water.

Joe McKiernan

Saved by the Bell

Look well to what surrounds you -
Look well,
For what you see and hear and smell
Are but the surface layer of life.
Beneath, are echoes of past livings,
Which now and then
Erupt through time's old years
And merge with our to-days and 'morrows.

I stand in the heart of Tallaght. Behind, I hear the buzz of shoppers, before me Rua Red - a centre for the arts, behind it the new library. Just opposite that the Civic Theatre, and behind all the layers of new flats and offices stands the hospital.

Everywhere the stimulation of the 21st century invades the air. I am swamped by endless lists of urgencies that regulate my life. My spirit's energy is dulled, confused with all the 'doings'.

Somewhere on the edge of consciousness a clanking bell splinters the numbness of my brain. The Luas tram slides gently to a halt – the terminus - its target, reached. And from its many openings flood living beings - pouring out and spreading – spreading like spilled blood.

The threads that join me to forgotten pasts tingle with life – and layers of years peal back to ancient times. The Tallaght of to-day fades from my eyes.

My vision is now filtered through with ancient colour – focussing I see thousands of people lying dead – slain by the army of Parthalon. The 'Annals of the Four Masters' tells us that, 5,000 years ago, before even the Fir Bolg or the Tuatha Dé Dannan, he and his followers, supposedly descendants of the Biblical Noah, invaded Ireland. They settled, and their industry and craftsmanship eventually transformed the countryside. I see it – right before my eyes - stone dwellings, cultivated land, cattle grazing in rich pastures. Then, as I'm absorbing this prosperity the vision fades. I once again see thousands of tortured dead littering the fields – but this time the enemy is imperceptible - it is the plague. History tells us that in one week alone nine thousand men and women died. Their burial ground is called Támh leacht - the plague burial ground. Today, it's known as Tallaght.

The scene before my eyes is heart-heavy; a pall of misery hanging over everything. For the few people that are left, life is pierced with loss, but anger is also there – anger against the gods and the Fomorians – the demonic peoples they believe have spread the killer-plague. This, in particular, is true of Tuan, son of Parthalon's brother Starn, who survives the pestilence. His anger lingers on, even past his death and, as the legends go, carries him through years of re-incarnation as an animal. Eventually his suffering is ended by Nuada's 'Sword of Light', but as he dies his curse of vengeance spews across the lands and people of Támhleacht.

From now 'till time is ended
The curse of Tuan, mighty warrior of Parthalon
Upon this place.
Each day, a long-and-shining-spear
Will pierce the heart of Thám leacht.
And from this open wound
Will gush forth darkness and distress
Upon its peoples.

    The scene around me shifts again and time has travelled on its course and woven change, but still the curse of Tuan blights the land. As was predicted, the people of Támh leacht are in daily torment from the curse of the long-and-shining-spear. A darkness hovers over everything. I see fields continually soaked with the blood of warriors - the daily onslaught of the curse killing the spirit of the people. Their pleadings to the great god Dagda reach out to emptiness. There is no hope alive within their hearts.
And then an answer comes, not from the ancient Celtic gods but from the new. A monastery of Christian monks is founded in this ancient place and daily the chapel bell of Maelruain calls man and woman and each child to prayer. Hope slowly enters in and over time it finds a home in people's hearts, and, as the seed of love replaces that of fear, the curse of Tuan starts to lose its power. Each day the long-and-shining-spear continues to invade their midst, but now the clang of chapel bell transforms the curse. And, from the former wounds of pain there now

begins to flow new life, prosperity and joy. The heart of Támh leacht has become a place renewed - a place of learning, healing, hope.

* * *

Startled by the clatter of a bell I find myself jerked back in time into the present moment. The heaviness of yester-years still clouds my mind. My vision of the ancient long-and- shining-spear re-focuses. I see the Luas tram, I hear the bell, I see the doors releasing floods of people – people spreading out – bringing healing, knowledge, life - right into the heart of Tallaght.

Ailish Massey

Small Gods in the Trees

Dar Green's driveway was filled with cars - slick black and silver things kissed red by the high summer sunset. Charlie jumped off her bicycle and manoevoured through to ring the doorbell. A man with obvious Eastern-European features answered, looking stunned by a teenage girl at the door. 'Is me Ma there?' She held her breath, expecting the door to be slammed or to be dragged in by the hair.
Earlier she'd been bouncing on a friend's trampoline, laughing through her starving belly when kids banged on the door. 'Your Ma's been taken,' they said. They circled and chased Charlie as she cycled home, like a pack of hyenas, giving her snips of information.
'She's dead, so dead. Dar's got her. Gone. Lost. Finished.'
Charlie heard fists hitting a punch bag. A second man appeared and spoke Polish to the first. They shouted into the house. Someone yelled back. The men ushered her in. The men went out to the back. Charlie could see a large shed. Loud R+B was playing. Inside the music deep masculine laughter, a muffled squeal and then silence.

Charlie was starving. She never had a set time for dinner, just the chance of some Smilie faces thrown into the microwave if she caught her mother at home. But her mother was always going out. Charlie had mostly stopped asking where. Charlie watched the men in the shed, backs rippling under tight t-shirts.

One of them stooped and she spotted her mother.
 She was waved at to come out.   The shed was built around an immaculate burgundy pool table. In the corner a Wurlitzer blazed neon, winding down the song she'd heard. Sitting beside it was her mother, tugging at her sleeve, kneading the flesh between her right elbow and wrist. She wouldn't make eye contact under the glare of the men. Between her mother and the men was an ashtray full of, fizzling coiled cigarettes. A bowl of chicken wings glistened and steamed on a table. Charlie swallowed.
'Howya,' a voice from behind, so treacly and intimate it brought hairs up on her neck. She turned to see a man with bright and gorgeous eyes. His hair was gelled and pristine, and he gazed at her with a sort of lusty appraisal, as if his whole life was about making young girls swoon. He offered his hand in introduction. When Charlie took it a swirling of déjà-vu came upon her, 'I'm Dar,' he said holding her hand. Charlie didn't answer. The world was woozy. Her eyes settled on the crumpled face of her mother. 'She's alright he said, she's just a bit stoned.'
Charlie ignored Dar. His amiable smile wavered.
'Did you not know your Ma was a junkie?'
Charlie knew, deep down. She'd been told. Called
names on the street. She never admitted it and so her denial was strong. She ignored Dar, and Dar's face darkened.'Ma?' Charlie said, her eyes on her mother, thinking look at me, please look at me. Dar reached for the food on the table. He bit into a wing and offered one to Charlie. She shook her head, saw the

dark in Dar's eyes, and shivered at the swirling feeling again.

'She's staying here.' Dar said and then to the mother. 'Aren't you?'

Everyone looked at Charlie's mother. She said nothing.

'She can follow you home later. Maybe. But as for you, you should go.'

'I'm not going without her,' said Charlie.

Her mother looked up, making eye contact once with her daughter, pain leapt from her eyes, and Charlie knew they were hurting her.

'It's a very stupid thing to do, to follow a doomed woman like you have,' Dar said.

'What?'

'Your mother's mine now. See. I take my job seriously but smackheads never do. I always end up having to prove myself. Your Ma understood the risks when she started buying from me. I have to take my payment whatever way I can.'

His face was a mask of sympathy.

'Is there any other way?'

'What's done is done,' said Dar.

'I'll do anything.'

Dar laughed loudly, the cronies nudged each other.

'You're a nice looking kid, and the first who's ever come here. So I'll give you one chance.' He stepped towards the cigarettes and took one up, blowing the ember to make it glow burning red. Charlie's mother flinched.

'You know the new hospital beside the Deadman's

Inn?' 'Course.' 'Well behind that there's a rapeseed field, and beyond that, bulrushes in flower. The seeds have a certain flavour I happen to love.' he said. There was a jar beside him on the table with a pliers standing up inside. He removed the pliers and replaced the lid before tossing it to Charlie. She heard a lone seed rattle as she caught it.

'If you can fill that jar with seeds and return before sunset, I'll let your mother free. And who knows - if you manage this, I'll find some other use for you too.'

Charlie wasn't sure he was serious. She looked at the men, and then Dar, expecting some sign of a joke. But the goon's eyes were dead, and Dar's eyes were intent and humourless.

'Will you accept this challenge?' He said.

The three men and her mother watched Charlie. She looked out at the reddening sky. She had no idea if Dar was telling the truth or simply distracting her, let alone whether she would actually be able to make it down to the valley and back, but she knew she had no choice. 'Yes,' Charlie said.

'So go. The quickest way is straight through the rapeseed field, cutting through the private hospital. Make sure you avoid the security guard though. He's mental.' Charlie ran outside and jumped onto her bike. The journey was quick, through an industrial estate where a cracked drainpipe spilled water to foster a profusion of dandelions on the broken pavement. The splashing water brought thoughts exploding in Charlie's mind. Her mother clean for a week last April, frantic to nurture things into growth. The living room a panic of just bought shrubs. Mother and daughter splashing water on newly planted wallflowers. Blackness rising in her mother's eyes, Charlie alone in the empty house, ignoring the flowers dying in the May sun.

Charlie reached the main road and crossed though a gap in the evening traffic. The hospital walls were huge. Charlie used the bike to boost herself, heaving it up after her before dropping down the other side.

***

The hospital was a radiance of steel and tempered glass with a garden spiralling around a central gazebo. By the gates Charlie could see the security hut, an unattended TV flickering in the shadows, and between the hospital and the hut, a tall balding man running towards her.

She jumped onto the bike and pedalled for the far wall, the man changed direction to intercept her. Charlie skidded to her left, losing her balance and falling from the bike before running on, barely escaping the man's grabbing arms. The back wall looked much higher than the one she'd already climbed. She tried anyway, her legs floundering as she clung to the top, devoid of any secure grip. The guard grabbed her, spun her around, slapped her, slammed her into the wall and shouted in her face spit hitting her cheeks. 'He sent you didn't he?'

'What?'

Slam
'That Greener scumbag!' *Slam*
'Well tell him I've had enough of you little scangers!
Slam slam slam
Charlie wanted to cradle her head but the guard held her arms, trying to catch his breath. He was missing an eye. He pointed at his scarred empty socket and yelled. 'That filth did this and then thinks he can send scum down here just to wind me up? And now this, a girl! You'll be so sorry he sent you,' he said. Charlie's t-shirt twisted in his fists, choking her, pushing her into the wall. She saw stars, felt her legs weakening until she kneed him hard once in the crotch.

He collapsed in a heap as if praying towards the wall. Charlie took a few steps back and vaulted using the guards back and head as a ramp. She scrambled over. Breeze blew yellow waves across the sashaying rapeseed field. She started running, stalks whipping against her hands, a greeny black wake behind her and a fine yellow dust peppering the air. She reached the forest. Instinct sharpened her hearing, quietened her breath. The ground felt mossy and soft. Bars of muted light brightened trees or cast ominous shadows. Spores tickled her nostrils. She jogged quickly on. White hemlock giving way to glossy ferns as the hillside grew treacherous, ever steeper and damper with the memory of the river in flood.She checked the jar in her pocket and listened for the guard, hearing chirps and the guttural crescendo of some unknown animal, the lap of the Liffey, the rustle

of leaves, the inimitable creak of tall swaying firs.
A blackbird squawked in alarm. Charlie stopped, listened. Feet crunched leaves nearby. She jumped to the ground. The panic of claustrophobia fluttered inside her, balanced by a fugitive's gratitude for cover. She waited, still, only moving when the guard was long gone. The night seemed to be seeping in faster now. She crawled along slowly, willing the last light to hold. She reached a cliff edge and slid down over stones decending through a grove of young sycamores before landing with a splat in cracking mud where the river had retreated. Sticking out from the mud like a fossil was a coke can, and beside it a small glimmering rock. She pulled it free of the mud and cleaned it. It was an ancient stone with a symbol etched into it. She put it in her pocket and looked for a way ahead but her way was blocked by bushes - tumultuous, uncontrollable rhododendrons. Knowing the river was right in front she ventured forward only to have branches wrap quickly around her legs, vines tangle up in her arms. Frustration overcame her, and again the feeling of déjà-vu. The more she fought the harder it became to move, each twist and pull seemed to draw more loops and spirals around her, arms and legs straining in the grip of the bushes, twisting, stretching. Scraped, she screamed when a branch snaked around her neck. As she choked, her eyes closed, and as she stopped struggling the bush released her and she slipped quietly into water below. Charlie didn't feel awake in the water. Instead she saw her mother, during a dawn at the very edge of

memory, before their slow and agonising drift apart. Her mother standing, glowing in the morning's first sunlight, her face guilty and vibrant before her habit took hold. In her hand she carried Wagon Wheels and a fizzy drink, every bubble a tiny sun. She sat on Charlie's bed and shook her four year old heel. The daughter rolled awake to see her mother's loving smile.

Charlie woke in a clearing. Purple clover closing. Jinny-joes floating in the twilit luminescence, tiny magnificent things as multitudinous as stars, and as the seeds touched her skin a whisper entered her mind.
Your mother is dead. All for nothing, she thought.
She heard movement, grass crunching, two thumps - the off-tempo rhythm of a man on a crutch.
She looked up to see a one legged man wearing a wretched looking duffle coat over an ancient tie-dyed hoodie. The hood was up and underneath the cowl his eyes sparkled. From his rusting crutch a set of bone coloured rosary beads hung, rattling as he moved.
'Story?' he said. 'I'm Ginty.
'Where am I?
'The Green belt of the soul. Take out your jar.'
Charlie took the jar from her pocket and shook it. A single tooth, not a seed rattled in the jar. 'That's your mother's,' said the man. 'Dar Green did the same to me.' He tapped a cruddy finger at his toothless lower gum. 'Many times.'
Charlie was distraught. On her knees. Her eyes glazed

with tears.'There's a chance to change things.'
'How? 'Our city is filled with edges, green overgrown places where those who seek cover can hide secrets and commit foul deeds. This is one such place. There are hundreds, thousands all over the city. Men and women have been left to rot in these places. Men like me. We are depleted souls who cannot cross over, staying behind to become the spring in the earth, the heat in the setting sun, the small gods in the trees.'
Charlie rubbed the rune stone in her pocket. Ginty tossed three more at her feet.
'One for each soul you must take for us.'
'What?'
'Dar Green has made this place his own. You're not the first he sent here, always destined to fail. He hides things here.'
'Like what?'
'Drugs and the dead. But there's an older essence here that follows the leylines of the past. It has given us power, and now is our time. The city is a machine choked with wickedness. A purge is coming. Will you help us?' Charlie sat motionless. Ginty spoke again.
'We can give you what you want.'The one thing Charlie wanted was her mother back.
Ginty answered before she put the wish into words. 'Time is a rippling tapestry; we can shake it out, remove or encourage a fold. But this will only provide the chance for your mother to change her mind at a certain point and that is all. If you join us

you will never know her decision and you will be bound to places like this, to the shadows that surround civilisation.' Charlie thought of April again, the evening with the flowers.
'Do it,' she said, and her head was thrown back, her breath taken. All the want within her and the repressed atoms of her love for her mother bloomed and exploded, exciting the forest that surrounded her into a furious motion. Her memories eroded, like the coast pulled under tides. She felt herself dissipated, but still conscious, joining a singular vibration, a vast organic rhizome of energy that infused every living thing.

In the shed, Dar Green and his men woke, déjà-vu in their heads and a stain in their hearts, a screaming guilt and emptiness that they frantically filled with daily binges of drugs and drink until the urge put them in a car that crashed, flipping once before exploding into flames on a Blanchardstown back road. Charlie was in the smoke, in the fire, in the last spin of the broken back wheels.
She lives on still, the shadow in the corner of bad men's eyes, the justice in a ricochet, the heart attack in an extra line, the magic in the dark that galvanises the good and is a banshee wail to the guilty.

Colm Keegan

Love Potion

Diarmuid was known throughout the west of Ireland as the little man of Coolavin. When he was born he was the smallest baby ever recorded. Niamh, his mother, had to knit and make all his clothes. Although he was small he was handsome, brave, fleet of foot and could hunt as well as any man. As an adult he stood just less than five feet. He lived with his mother in a little cottage on the shores of Lough Gara.

One day while at the Horse Fair in Ballinasloe he saw a beautiful dark haired girl across the market square. His friend Pakie jokingly encouraged him to talk to her. Compared to Diarmuid she was a giant at six foot. So he mustered up all his courage and spoke to her.

'My name is Diarmuid,' he said, 'and you are the most beautiful girl I ever saw.' She looked down at him from her great height.

'Well Diarmuid, my name is Saoirse and tell me, am I talking to the little man of Coolavin?'

'Aye that's me'.'Will you be at the dance later on tonight?' he asked.

'I will indeed.'

'Sure I'll see you there.' They danced all night, she was very impressed with his jigs and reels. A couple of months later he asked her to marry him and she happily agreed. He brought her home to Lough Gara. They were very happy for a while. But soon she started complaining.'Oh Diarmuid that cow is too big

I can't milk her.' So he would do it himself. Then she claimed that the chickens would attack her everytime she went to feed them or the fairies turned the butter when she churned it. Poor Diarmuid had to do all the work as she grew fatter and lazier. She moaned and complained to him all the time and made his life hell.

One day he rowed his boat out to the middle of the lake just to get a bit of peace and quiet. He could still hear roaring from the shore, telling him what she thought of him. He caught a big trout and decided to row to the island to cook and eat it. As night fell he built himself a shelter and went to sleep. He was woken by mystical music and followed the sound. To his surprise he came upon a tribe of little people dancing and singing in the moonlight. He was enchanted by one little person, she wore a pink dress and a crown of sparkling diamonds. She introduced herself as Neysa, Queen of the tiny people.

'You look very sad,' she said. Diarmuid told her of his harridan of a wife.

'Why don't you stay here with us?' she asked.

Diarmuid decided there and then to do just that. Soon he and Neysa fell in love. Life was great. They sang and danced all day long,both of them were so happy. After three years he decided to go visit his mother. Neysa warned him to be back before the sun rose. Otherwise he would not be able to find the island again. He promised he'd be back in plenty of time. But when he landed on the shore Saoirse was waiting.

'So you've come back,' she said.'I've come to visit my mother.' 'Well you better hurry she's not well. Go on up to the house, I'll look after your boat.'

When he had gone she got the biggest boulder she could find and smashed it into the bottom of the boat rendering it useless. Meanwhile Neysa was waiting. When he did not return she got on her butterfly and flew to land. She saw the boat and knew he could not return to her. She could not live without him and consulted the elders, who told her she would have to find a new place for them to live. She travels to the future to the time of King Arthur. She tells her story to Merlin the famous wizard. He takes pity on her and gives her a recipe for a potion. She must travel to Mars to collect dust. As Mars is the God of War this will make him strong like a warrior. On to Venus as she is the Goddess of Love to catch some moonbeams. This will strengthen his love. Next to middle earth, where a group of mole like people called Trogites live. They spend their lives tunnelling into the earth's core. They release the water that creates the rivers, streams and wells. From the Trogites she gets the purest, softest, coldest water from the fountain of life. At the hill of Tara she found the best toadstools. St Patrick gave her his freshest shamrock. Next she went to ancient Greece where Zeus himelf made her a special potion.Then she returned to Lough Gara and took Diarmuid to Tallaght far away from Saoirse. At the townland of Tymon she planted the toadstools and some of the shamrock. Immediately a fairy fort sprung up. The dust from Mars and the moonbeams from Venus she mixed with shamrock and water from middle earth. This magical mixture she administered to Diarmuid. Before her eyes he changed into a tiny creature like herself. She brought him to the fairy fort. She then drank the potion Zeus had given her. Now she too could live away from her mystical island. That is why to this day people are reluctant to damage or destroy a fairy fort, for fear of disturbing Neysa and her true love Diarmuid.

Genevieve Greene

Send for the Swans

On the largest Crannog in the centre of Lough Tymon, amid enchanted Wicklow hills, the Druids sit. Time stands still as their minds lock with the Goddess Danu. Together they search the universe for the immortals. One of the four talisman of great power has been stolen by invaders. Their magic protection has been weakened and they alone cannot find the flaw. In the ring of living beauty circling the innermost chamber, the great spinning wheel, and the all-seeing eye, has suddenly lost all power.

Music from the golden waterfall has started to fade, becoming a thin trickle of whispers like dead leaves floating in the wind. Stone scarabs leer, while moonstones wink wearily. Mermaids swim listless among the coral beds, their shining tails growing dim. The hanging gardens of the great Tymon Castle are starting to crumble. The humans are breaking through, things are falling apart, Milesian tribes are no longer content to share the kingdom.

At last word has reached the gods on the very edge of the universe itself. The golden eagle of Tylough is huge as befits a god of mighty stature. His plumage is shot through with bronze and copper. When he opens his powerful wings he is a fearful sight. He roams the planets and stars, great black eyes searching every world for his partner, (The Goddess Mon). Swift as an arrow she swims through oceans of time and space to be at his side for the final battle. A mermaid of such beauty it was said that if any mortal man laid eyes on her, he would be blinded forever. Together they will save their brethren the Sidhe. They will leave behind the best and wisest, to guide mortals from the dark. And so it happened as they decreed.

Word went out to the Salmon of Knowledge, 'Send for the Swans.' On that day a great meeting took place on the lough. The great God Tylough and the Goddess Mon waited as four great swans came wheeling in a great arc around the lake. All at once there was a hush, the sun and moon shone and a gentle breeze ruffled the water as in a blinding flash four mortal children stood like golden statues. The children of Jedward had come home. An evil Lord called Simon De Cowell, jealous of their golden hair had unleashed music so powerful it turned them into swans. All at once there was music everywhere, and the golden boys went among the mortals singing songs of peace. And the legend said, that was the day boy bands started, as they threw away their old clubs and picked up guitars.

Then it was time for the Sidhe to leave their homeland forever. A great silver ship took them away to an island called *Celebrity Forever*. There it is said they will never grow old. The great lake of Tymon and the castle still lie under the enchanted mountains. And some dark misty nights when mortals lie in bed a mermaid swims again, while on the castle wall a stone eagle forever watches.

Aine Lyons

Silver Willow

The old crone, who put into place the spell, walked slowly up to the castle where they both lived. Three loud knocks echoed through the great hall as the two young lovers stood, waiting. Holding on to each other they remembered, vividly, how their union came to be and how the old crone held court when the King of the Land and the King of the Sea came together to settle once and for all the long feud that had been going on for many years.

For as long as people could remember the King of the Land, Rí na Tíra, sat on the high throne of Ireland. He declared himself King of all Kings in all the lands. He ruled from his castle in Coill an Rí, Kingswood. But he was a cruel King. Not satisfied with all the terror he inflicted on his country, he decided to invade lands across the sea. He ordered that the tall trees of the forest be felled and that some kind of vessel be built. It needed to be strong enough to last the journey.

In his arrogance the King never asked permission of the King of the Sea to enter his domain. He ordered his ships plunge into the sea and roared at his terrified army. These were land people and most of them had never set foot in the sea. They knew of the stories of the fierce King of the Sea. He was equal to their own King in strength and bravery. People lined the shore to watch their loved one leave the safety of the land as the huge number of ships set out on their voyage. They cried and prayed to the gods for protection and forgiveness for such a foolish King.

A furious Rí na Farraige rose up from the depths. Waves crashed over the ships causing some of them to turn and sink to the bottom. 'Who dares to enter my Kingdom?' he roared, thrashing and punching the water. Rí na Tíra stood at the helm of his ship and with all the fierceness he could muster he roared, 'I am King of all the land of Ireland and you should bow down before me.'

'Why should I?' the King of the Sea asked. 'You need my permission to enter my sea. You need me to grant you safe passage. King of Kings you may be on land but not in my domain.'

Fierce battles raged for many years. People lost their lives on land and in the sea. Nothing was ever gained and so much was lost, by everyone. After a long time the King of the Sea and the King of the Land saw reason. They had both learned the folly of war. So the seas calmed and the great ships returned to the shore.

To seal the agreement they sought the council of the oldest, wisest crone in the world. She made them form a pact to create the peace that everyone had longed for so long. She asked for only one thing from each King. To give up the most precious thing that they possessed.The King of the Sea gave up his daughter. The King of the Land gave up his son.

In an old crackled voice she declared, for all to hear, 'Let them be joined forever. Let nothing or no-one come between them. You must both agree to keep the peace between the land and the sea. There must be no breaking of this spell. No reason given will be good enough. You will lose everything. Do you both agree?' she asked. Then she went about the business of creating the most powerful spell she could. She called to the sea. From its depths came the most beautiful mermaid. Her hair was long and flowing. Green, blue, silver colours cascaded from her head. Her body was soft and supple. Her tail was the same colours as the sea. Her beauty was like nothing ever seen on the land. She then called for the son of the King of the Land to come forth from the thick forests. He was tall and slender. He had silver blond hair and his blue eyes were set in a handsome face. He was fit and strong and was wise beyond his years.

When the young prince saw the beautiful mermaid his heart was lost to her forever. She vowed to stay to him forever too. This was very unexpected. Love was never part of the spell. The pact was sealed. The two young lovers would stay together, forever.

But, as with all Kings, agreements never last. The land people grew angry when the sea flooded their fields and made the crops fail. The sea people also grew angry when the people of the land threw their rubbish into the water and poisoned them, causing their people to become ill. Tempers flared and egos grew bigger as each side wanted revenge.

The crone pushed the huge wooden doors open slowly. She stood with the Staff of the Sea in her left hand and the Staff of the Land in her right hand. Digging deep into the earth she drew a circle around the frightened couple. A tremendous noise was heard far and wide. Thunder crashed and lightening lit up the black sky. Rain crashed onto the land and the sea. When a mighty spell was broken it would rain for forty days and forty nights. The two young lovers clung to each other, vowing never to let go. The crone asked if they wished to say anything before she set into place all that had been agreed. That they should never see each other again. Raising the two Staffs and crossing them over their heads she whispered her spell. They kissed and smiled for one last time. Then they thanked the crone, 'you have given us a treasure that we never thought we would have. A love so strong, it will last forever.'

She interrupted the rhythm of the spell which caused a tremor to run through the castle. No one had ever thanked her. 'I cannot break the terms of an agreement,' she hissed, 'you must never see each other again. You must return to the sea,' she said, pointing to the young mermaid princess and you, young prince, you must stay on the land.'

The tears of the princess fell, making a pool around her feet. 'Please help us,' she begged. For the first time in history of witches and crones the terms were bent but not broken. Standing back to back, holding hands, the princess was turned into a willow. Her long flowing hair blowing in the wind slowly turned into branches. Her willowy body, slim legs and feet stood together in her pool of salty tears. Her lover, her prince, stood with his back to her. His tall body and long limbs turned, slowly, painfully, into a birch tree. His silver blond hair was to be the colour of every birch tree in the future centuries. They both blended into each other, becoming one for all time.

In the wild winds of winter he would give her strength and protection and she would blend with him as they supported each other. Their vow held true. They stayed together forever. When the rain stopped, the people of the sea and the land lamented for the couple. The magnificent castle was now in ruins as the foundations gave way to the flood waters, the remains of which can be seen today.

It's a special place, known as Coill an Rí. A hallowed place where strange things happen. Where two worlds come together. A place where young lovers meet and carve their names into the trees that grow there. Over the years, people young and old, return to find their sweetheart's tree and retrace their initials. Not all survive, only the initials of true loved ones are as fresh as when they were first carved.

In this quiet place, where the sound is the rustle of the leaves blowing in the breeze or the hushed sound of the Luas tram as it rushes by, not everyone knows the history of Coill an Rí. But on empty dark nights, when the full moon casts a shadow over the silver willow that grows there, if you are lucky, you might hear the mermaid's song of true love.

Patricia Verdon

Snowdrop

In the forests of Montpelier 2,000 years after the *'Fianna'* roamed the Glenasmole Valley; a god named Colias arrived from Sobul. His companion was a papilio called Indra. Indra was a magnificent butterfly-like creature with swallow tail wings that turned into a golden ball in flight. He had been with Colias from the beginning of time, illuminating the worlds of darkness in Sobul with his hypnotic golden beam and was fated as his trusted guide on this path of destiny.

When Colias entered the forest, the sounds reminded him of home, wind whispering through the leaves, distant streams, insects buzzing, creatures warning each other of intrusion. Colias made little or no sound as he followed his guide, the tree bodies creaking after him, oak eyes fixed on both of them.

They soon reached an opening surrounded by barren trees; rising to great heights they framed the sky like the eye of a cave. Indra rose spreading his beam of light, the dead russet branches growing lush green leaves quickly followed by berries the colour of carmine and corolla petals of ghost wings. The wings grew and grew surrounding Colias like an enormous world cloud. He could see Indra above him as he allowed himself be seduced by the circle of dream. The music within it, one of beauty and sweetness, called the song thrushes from the forest. The birds formed a mat beneath Colias and brought him out of the darkness into a whitened blue sky. He travelled north over a lush valley with steep drifts on either side and woodlands of hazel bellowing down to an ancient stream. The song thrushes finally led him to a meadow of ruby poppies and clusters of bright yellow monkey flowers each stained with blood drop emlets, as if the poppies were metamorphosing them into surrender.

Colias could see Indra ahead fighting the lips of the monkey flowers that sniped at his wings. The circle of dream scattered as Colias, regaining his earthly awareness, looked around him. Then he saw her. Beyond the sea of wild flowers, a magnificent red creature with tiny snowdrops above her eyes. It had been a long time since Colias had seen a deer and certainly never one of such beauty. She was swift and nimble, with an air of unpredictability about her; her black diamond eyes stared across the meadow, sensing a difference.

When she turned to retreat, the petals of the wild flowers closed behind her. Colias wasted no time following her, the speed of his movement gaining pace with the intake of the breeze; Indra freeing himself from the monkey flowers flew towards him as they both watched the graceful animal head for the stream. Once there she slowed, carefully crossing on a path of stones, ensuring none of her touched the water. When Colias reached the stream, his instincts told him to do the same, and once safely on the other side, himself and Indra entered the hazel forest.

He could see her up ahead; she travelled with the instinct of centuries. It was only when Colias saw the crystal kingdom shining out from the earth's core that he knew he had met his destiny. Once the red deer passed the crystal wall, she transformed into a goddess of wild red waist length hair and cotton skin draped by liquid gold. Around her forehead remained the snowdrops, only dimmed by her eyes of black lagoons. Inside the Crystal Kingdom, the earthly world was no longer part of her and although Colias and Indra were able to see in, they had no means of gaining entry. Indra in his vain attempts to enter became impatient when his wings started to fade. Colias was more resolute, the imaginings of his dreams had finally been realised and it was just a question of time.

* * *

Makaylah was soon joined in the crystals by Edana, the goddess of fire transformed from a wild cat. Her hair was black like the raven with a garland of large red roses around her forehead. With skin darker than Makaylah's she wore a dress in blood red, revealing womanly curves that held the power of all men's passions. An ice fox was the next to arrive and just like Makaylah she turned into a creature so beautiful she had no need for any crown. The iced white of her coat became long straight hair of purple silk with lips to match. Kindall may not have had the purity of Makaylah or the full bodied passion of Edana, but she was indeed a clever, independent fox.
'Ah, Kindall, you are just in time, Makaylah here

thinks she's seen him.'

'Seen who?'

'The warning of her forefathers, the creature she must never kiss.' Edana lets out an infectious laugh just as Peigi arrives.

'Makaylah has seen him?' the white dove becoming the last of the sisters to transform.

Makaylah looks at Peigi, the youngest of them all; the colour of the oceans in her eyes, her wings now a headdress of three circles in white weave, the centre piece laced in crystals like her dress. She has a beauty so magical that it sets her apart, even from her sisters.

'Heavens Makaylah, is this true? You have finally met him?' Peigi swoons.

'Do you not get it Peigi, '*romance*', not that I normally resist the absolute divine delight of it, is completely out of the question here.'

'Edana, maybe the warning is wrong, this creature might be her true love.'

But Peigi concedes defeat when Kindall speaks.

'She cannot afford to take a chance.'

Makaylah looking at her three sisters remembers Colias as he stood in the meadow. Each of them can see the vision in her eyes; they feel her deepest emotions, knowing he is within her like the centre stones of earth.

It is Kindall that speaks next. 'Makaylah you know if you kiss him, you will go to the Valley of Darkness?'

'I know; everything from my creation to now

confirms what you say, but even though I understand this, there is something drawing me to him.'

'Absolutely darling, the more passionate and tempting they seem, the more one should be wary, unless of course you like to live dangerously like me?'

'I think Makaylah should go to the Forest of Answers,' says Peigi.

'Will you take me there sweet Peigi?'

'Of course I will, but we must sleep now, tomorrow before daylight we will go. The gods might give you answers in your dreams.'

When Makaylah awakes her sad eyes tell Peigi nothing has changed. Peigi transforms herself into her earthly dove form and Makaylah on her back shrinks to the size of the most minuscule of fairies. They fly to the Forest of Answers unaware that in their wake follows the daring Colias.

The Forest of Answers is chilled with white earth and tall brittle trees covered by emerald moss. Makaylah and Peigi stand as goddesses, calling to the forest, but it is over the spirit of Makaylah that the light comes. Finjela the mythical daughter of Oisin rises from nothing; no face at first and with long feathered wings that spread like a peacock consuming the light; behind her ambers of richness glow.

'Dear Makaylah,' she whispers from above, 'do you not know that he is here to take the light from you, that the snowdrops that protect you are his only means of bringing Sobul out of darkness. If you go with him, like my father you will take earthly form.'

Colias and Indra having followed the glow of Finjela arrive as she issues her last warning.

'Makaylah,' says Colias, 'if you come with me I will protect you.'

'Brave Colias; do you want her to die for you? What price are you prepared to pay?' asks Finjela.

'I would die for her in an instant.'

Finjela spreads out her hands across the white earth and creates a pool into the future. Colias and Makaylah are both standing barefoot in the Forbidden Stream, the white snowdrops around Makaylah's head rise and are absorbed into the golden ball of Indra.

'What does this mean Finjela?' pleads the soft voice of Peigi.

'It means this is their destiny; should they choose it.'

Both of them know they have no choice.

At the Forbidden Stream they each follow the vision, placing their bare feet in the dangerous water. The white snowdrops rise into the golden ball just as they had seen and Colias bids farewell to his lifelong friend.

As Indra sets off to the Kingdom of Sobul, the two kiss and both Colias and Makaylah feel the force of the centuries rise and empty all godliness from them. Within moments they turn into their earthly forms, Makaylah the deer, one small snowdrop remaining on her forehead and Colias transforming into the body of the Great Irish Elk, his antlers giving him the height of a grown man.

Now when you roam the Glenasmole Valley, you will still find Makaylah and Colias wandering in the forests or bathing down by the stream. Look out for the snowdrop, it never left her.

Louise Phillips

The Sweet Breath of Deception

'Ah Wife, Wife, why have you sought to fool me? Did you think to slip unnoticed a mewling mortal child into the pure warrior cast of Phallorian's seed?'

The air vibrated with Phallorian's anger. He stood at the entrance of the Labyrinth and the echo of his multiple voices bounced throughout the surrounding forest. It was but one of his godly powers. Each time he spoke, the King's voice came forth with myriad sibilant hissing sounds. If the listener had nothing to fear, then just one voice was heard; but if you were the enemy or if wrong had been done, the other voices cut like knife blades through the tender layers of the hearing globes, ripping the thought processes to bloody jagged shreds.

Pea, his wife, fell to the ground, groaning with the pain his voice inflicted.

'Please my Lord, my King, not the voices, please!'

She folded her delicate little winglet handies over the tiny globes at each side of her head. At the same time she displayed her perfect haunches to him hoping that the stardust scattering of golden fur would have its usual effect.

'NOOOOOO!' her husband roared. 'You will not seduce me away from this! This thing that you have done to me, to us, will dilute forever our powers, the strength of our dominance here in this teetering world. You weakling! You and that foolish orgiastic tingling of the loins over which you have no control! Somewhere in your ancestry must lurk a pallid human conception. Pah!'

The huge warrior king, half-man half-beast encased in bony breastplate, spat in contempt.

'Bring me the newborn creature,' he commanded.

'No, no, you shall not have him, you shall not hurt him, he is mine, of me!'

But Phallorian strode to the basket on the ground behind his wife and plucked the child from within, holding it aloft above the flames of the eternal fire.

A surge of beings skittered in from the edges of the forest, hissing and babbling. The rag-tag horde of half-hoofed, part-furred, metaled and scaly life-forms advanced towards their acknowledged Chieftain.

Pea moaned piteously. The baby boy that Phallorian held was large by human standards but by the mores of the Phultaeous Tribe he was but a scrap, a shameful Halfling, devoid of special strengths or powers. A limp, pink-skinned cross-breed.

Suddenly there appeared Scabyrous, maniacal second son of Phallorian and Pea. He danced wildly beside his father in his favourite guise of upright lizard, striking ice into Pea's heart. Scabyrous had the power to change his appearance and fluctuated madly between lizard, boar, giant stoat, or serpent – whatever suited his malevolent mood.

'Drop him in the fire, Dada! Into the fire with the imposter, let him roast and bubble! He is contagious, he will contaminate our world. Burn him, burn him, Dada!'

'No, Phallorian,' Pea screamed. 'I beg of you, he did nothing wrong, punish me! But let the child live.'

'What hume-ling half-wit did you couple with to produce him?' Phallorian roared. 'Where did you find this specimen who outstrips me in the procreation game? ANSWER ME!'

'I flew to a green country,' his wife sobbed, 'whose people sang and danced. Where they did not fight but loved. I drank of their mead, their music and their men and I drank of their gentle ways.'

'Are you telling me Wife, that *THEY WERE LEGION*? That you can not remember who has fathered this abomination upon you? I WILL NOT BE SO SHAMED! I will not give safe harbor to this alien!'

And Phallorian shook the child so hard over the fire that his swaddling garments fell off and melted into the flames below. A gasp rose up from the watchers. Realising the child was naked, Phallorian lowered him down to eye level and inspected him closely, turning him this way and that.

'I can see no godlike features, no nubs of latent wings or horns, no tracery of carapace to come. What did he get from you? What are his strengths, his special powers? What can he do in this world?'

'He blows a sweet breath, my Lord, so sweet it can make the wheat fields grow and golden orchards spring up in an instant and clear contagion from the lungs of man.'

'Then he must go to where such puny strengths are admired for they will be of no use to him here in the land of the Phultaeousian'. Phallorian tucked the child violently into his breastplate, as if he were a baby rabbit.

'Bring me my Pegasus, my trusty carrier! Come wife, you and I and your misbegotten whelp will retrace your steps to this place from whence you debauched yourself, what is it called?'

'Newcastle,' said Pea.

Aboard the broad hairy back of Pegasus, Phallorian, Pea and the child soared upwards and flew swooping and diving over the mountains and seas till they came within sight of the townland of Newcastle in the County of Dublin, in the land of Eire.

Hovering low, Phallorian steadied his steed and, reaching inside his breastplate, withdrew the squirming child.

'No, No! Phallorian, please don't,' Pea begged for her child's life.

But Phallorian, cackling into the air with his voice of a thousand blades, dropped the babe earthwards through thunder and lightening and turned his steed around.

Pea struggled to loosen the grip of her husband's horny tail. They twisted and fought together in the air, with the feisty beast flailing beneath them.

'Let me go to my child!' she cried.

Phallorian uncoiled his tail, ripping Pea's wings as he did so and sent her plummeting earthwards to land in the soft rich soil of Newcastle. The breath was plucked from her lungs and she lay as dead.

Now it so happened that five fields away from where his mother lay, the Halfling babe, let's call him Ornery, was growing prodigiously fast in the human atmosphere which suited him well. He dwelt amongst the people of Baldonnel. His little singing breaths had spewed and planted vast and swift growing orchards of apples and pears of delicious perfection. His eating of them soon had him walking on sturdy legs through the fields.

From the depths of a wheat field the child heard a pitiful moaning and running through the high yellow sea of waves he came upon his own beautiful mother, her tiny feathery wings broken beyond repair and the breath in her lungs damaged and sour.

He had a memory of hearing her voice.

'He blows a sweet breath, my Lord, so sweet it can make golden wheat fields grow, and lush orchards spring up in an instant and clear contagion from the lungs of man.'

And with his human love and his heavenly power Ornery blew the fresh clear air from his own lungs straight into his mother Pea. And kindly humans who had gathered round were amazed. They embraced the felled and homeless godlings and named their land of plenty and healing, Peamount.

Joan Power

Tallaght Deer and the Goddess Ceres

Sean Walsh Park, now a place where the good people of Tallaght may go during the daylight hours, was not always a scrap of land, well mowed, manicured and maintained as it is, between The Square Shopping Centre, Old Bawn and Aylesbury.

The park, many years ago, was simply an extension of the Dublin hills, sparsely inhabited by humans but with a wide variety of plant and animal life. Many deer stalked the area. They were unafraid of humans, as they were so few. Deer had the run of the land, springing graceful over the hills and bogs, from the flat lands up to the crests of the hills, over to places like Three Rock and as far as Kippure.

Over many thousands of years the land became more densely populated by man. They brought with them their habits and traditions, and they built houses. They grew their own food and prayed for a good harvest each year, so that their families would stay healthy and prosper.

One of the many gods these primitive people worshipped was Ceres. She was Goddess of Agriculture, grain and the love a mother bears her child. Ceres was good to the people of Tallaght, they did indeed prosper but the deer had started to retreat. They were driven up into the hills due to fear of humans but also because their natural habitat was beginning to disappear. The deer became timid and avoided contact with man. Deer can be seen on the hills above Tallaght, but these sightings are fortuitous and fleeting, as the deer confine themselves to places where human feet rarely tread. That is on every day of the year apart from one, the feast day of Ceres, sometimes called 'Cerealia' on the 19th April. On this day, deer have been spotted in Sean Walsh Park. It is said that Goddess Ceres granted the deer the freedom of the park, without fear of danger, on this one day of the year. They travel down from the hills to give thanks that they have survived the intrusion of man onto their ancestral lands and for their undisturbed habitat on the hills above Tallaght.

Grace Moore

The Black Plague

King Connor was standing at the battlement of his castle, the very same castle in which the ruins remain today in the heart of Tallaght. He was weary and battle sore and blood ran into his eyes from a deep incision an enemy blade had opened in his forehead. The pain he was feeling was not from his wound, but coming deep within his heart. His men courageous in battle were just no match for this superior foe. They out-matched his branch of warriors in every way possible. Leinster had, under his reign, endured peace and prosperity over the last twenty years and no one in the land had come to challenge his throne, not until now.

Rage now replaced anger and that anger he directed at himself for letting his warriors become soft and not hardened for battle. Mixed emotions stirred within him as he helplessly watched his men being slaughtered all around him. How could he ever defeat such a foe? They had bronze weapons but the enemy had weapons that were stronger and by far sharper. They used these weapons with such ease and skill, not even his best warriors could come close to matching. He knew as he watched, his people would never defeat such an enemy in the heart of battle. His decision was not an easy one but he had no alternative. He knew when he made this decision there would be no going back. He couldn't dabble with the other world and not eventually pay a price. That night under the cover of darkness he and two of his best warriors set out in the direction of the Dublin hills. Little he knew of the person he was seeking, but stories had filtered down to him and he was not sure which was legend and which was true. People wondered was she a real woman or just took shape of one? Some had remarked, she was stunningly beautiful and some claimed horrifically ugly. He would now find out as he crept silently through the trees and made his way to the cabin door. He was startled to find a person who looked old and frail and was sitting at a big welcoming fire. As though she could read his mind, she retorted 'don't be deceived by appearances my mighty King. I never thought the mighty King of Leinster would come seeking my help no matter how desperate he should be.'

'You seem to know so much, so do you know my enemy?' he asked. She simply replied 'of course, they were once enemies of mine.'

'Your enemy is a prince by the name of Parthalon. He comes from a far away land known as Greece.' She began to explain that in the same way the Irish had their pagan gods, the Greeks had their gods as well. She told the king of a god by the name of Zeus and how he had a son by the name of Pan. His son was a mischievous son and was never governed by the laws of the gods. Forbidden it was to fall in love with a mortal in which he did. His father then set out to destroy this mortal. He was unable to however, as Pan interceded and begged his father not to. She was exiled to a far away land and never to return. It was now obvious to her why Parthalon was here, it was to seek her out and kill her for she possessed similar powers to Pan. She had made love to Pan on the night of her exile and from that night forward her life was never the same as she became possessed and driven by the powers she somehow inherited from the God Pan.

'I will destroy your enemy,' she told him with vengeance in her heart. 'Do not go near the river Dodder for the next two weeks,' she ordered the king who left, puzzled and bewildered.

Parthalon and his band of warriors arose somewhat enchanted and enticed to a sweet smell coming from the local river, the Dodder. As they drew near they could not help themselves from being drawn to the sweet aroma coming from it. On gazing upon the river they were spellbound by the magical wonder that flowed in front of their very eyes. The river was a beautiful liquid of black mixing with a current of rippling cream. The smell was overwhelming of barley and hops. So strong was the spell's influence the men dived straight into the river and gorged themselves in the black liquid almost to the point of drowning. On the third day they were so intoxicated by the mysterious water that King Connor when entering their encampment did not know whether to slay his enemy or dance with them, such was their merriment.

It was said that nine thousand of Parthalon's men were slaughtered that day but ironically died laughing. It is also said this is how Tallaght got its name as Taim Leacht translated in English means the plague grave. It is also rumoured that the old lady from the cabin is an ancestor of Arthur Guinness but then again who would believe such stories as now it is said the cabin is also known as the Hell Fire Club and on hearing of the mysterious death of its occupant Pan himself appeared with the hooves and horns of a goat.

People mistook him as the devil, but he was just his mischievous self paying his respects to an old lover.

Robert Dowdall

The Gift of Dance

In the beginning of time all humankind knew how to fly. It was a divine right to be able to soar above the earth with the birds. The strong and proud people of South Dublin glided through the skies, warmed in the ever shifting golden light that chased the shadows across the Tallaght hills. This gift was given by the Creator in order for his children to come close to him whenever he called, his voice breaking the stillness in the Tymon woodland, rippling the cool water of the Dodder, and stirring the grassy fields of the Griffeen Valley.

As decades swelled to centuries, his beloved children became more fascinated with foolish pleasures and wandering in the vast and lush lands than finding contentment and happiness in answering his calls. Like the wily red fox that dashes through mossy fallen logs and secrets himself, they hid from their Creator, ignoring his urgent calls and pretending not to hear the cadences of his voice. So, inevitably, the Creator grew angry and punished his children by taking back the gift of flight.

Soon his children become bored and lonely roaming the fields and hills. They had become isolated from each other and grew fearful. No longer did they know the joy of soaring over Glen na Smol, feeling the air rush through their hair, close enough to touch the blue of gossamer clouds. They beat on drums made from goatskin so that the Creator might hear them. In their panic, the pounding grew more frantic, throbbing, frantic beats matching those of their own hearts. The reverberations shook the holly and blackberry bushes that lined the deer trails in the forest pathways of Kiltipper, tapped off the weathered and scarred bark on the mighty obeech trees in Tymon and swayed the windblown muted yellow and gold fields of Brittas. In vain, the people kicked up their legs and wildly thrust their arms but could not fly to their Master's side.

Looking down at his beloved children and watching their futile struggle to leave the ground and reach him, compassion swelled inside his chest. He transformed their movements into dance to replace what he had taken in removing their ability to fly. He erased all memories of flight from their minds, replacing them with feelings of joy in the movement of the dance.

The Creator knew in his infinite wisdom, that his children needed more than the gift of dance to find contentment and be fulfilled. He declared that the lands of South Dublin would thrive and prosper. Over time, his children would unite and form clans living within the pristine wild lands. Year after year, as moss slowly crept up and attached itself to the aging stone walls of St Maelruain's, villages would emerge and expand with roads and buildings reaching toward the sky and weaving across the landscape like the glossy deep green ivy that hugs the sycamore and ash trees of Corkagh Demesne and Tymon Park. Places of learning would drive out ignorance and fear in the hearts and minds of people. Centres of healing for the mind, body and spirit would evolve and help those in need. The Creator's children would come together to celebrate the arts and rejoice in their talents. All these places would serve them well and help to heal the wounds that famine, plague and poverty create. In time more of his children would migrate from far off lands and settle, making the community as rich and diverse as the multicoloured wildflower meadows that spread across the banks of the River Camac.

The Creator's command that the landscape of South Dublin will continue to evolve while its people remain strong, proud, and humble before him still exists today. The gift of joy and celebration through dance will live on for all time, connecting them to their loving Creator who dwells within the skies above his beloved South Dublin.

Ann Cullen

The Hermitage

Many a moonlit night walking along Fortification Hill, I stand and listen to the trees swaying and the lyre playing. I swear I even hear poetry being read. I'm not surprised, because the tale has it that the spirit of Orpheus, the most famous poet and musician who ever lived, is everywhere here.

Orpheus, the most gifted man in Greece goes to pieces when Eurydice dies. He seeks out Hades, a master of optical illusions. Hades is only too delighted to see this much loved man suffer and plays a cruel trick on him. Orpheus ends up so devastated he brings his sorrow into every walk of life. The wind tries whispering in his ear but he's so wrapped up in himself he hears nothing. It's only when the Maenads tear him apart limb from limb and the Muses make him whole again that he decides to leave Greece. With two of his strongest slaves he sets sail, not caring where he goes. Apollo comes to his rescue many times on his long and hazardous journey. He calms the stormy seas and when mountains spit fire on Orpheus, the sea quenches the flames.

After several days at sea they make a dreadful discovery. A stowaway is on board. Dragged from the hull is a desolate creature, weak with hunger.
'Who are you?' asks Orpheus.
'I'm Enda, your slave my Lord. The Lady Eurydice favoured me and now I can't live without her. I beseech you have mercy on me, my Lord.'

For seven years and a day he sails, following the

Sun God. When the sun shines so brightly and so long in the sky, Orpheus decides this is where he will land. A large grey dog suddenly appears at his feet. Orpheus is mesmerized. The dog speaks.

'My name is Faolain, I'm a Wolfhound. Rest here, then I will guide you.'

Orpheus is too stunned to do anything especially when he sees a flock of swans making a beautiful descent. They sing, 'we are the children of Lir and we welcome you to our land. Stay and prosper and when our curse is lifted we shall join you. Until then we shall talk through the wind.'

Stunned, he follows Faolain faithfully until they come to the foot of a mountain with a view of the sea. Here grass grows high and among the many trees animals strut and dance. A plant with three leaves on each stem grows everywhere. Yellow and blue flowers decorate the banks along pathways and their aroma fills the air. There's an abundance of fruit and vegetables never tasted before. They eat their fill, and a small stream where salmon leap high supplies all their drinking needs. For the first time in years Orpheus is content and his sweet music fills the air. When he plays, deer and boar stand side by side as do fox and the hens, the stoat and the badger. The hedgehog refuses to needle anyone as he sits on the white horse's back.

Wandering one night with Faolain he comes across a family of little people. They are so small they're nearly invisible. It's the light of the moon shining on them that attracts his attention. His lyre is in his hands and playing. Before long these wee folk are dancing and singing to his music. They accompany him on what they call a harp. He's enchanted with them and they spend the night exchanging stories. He learns this is their land called Ringfort or Rathfarnham. He's free to live among them and join them any night. The only condition they make is he's to tell no-one of their existence. Having learned his lesson years ago he's able to promise them faithfully he'll do all in his power to protect them.

Watching the animals so happy he starts to feel guilty about his slaves. It doesn't seem right that his companions should not be as free as the animals. Calling them together he blesses them all and tells them he has no further use of them and they are free. Enda, who looked after his every need, cries and begs to be allowed to stay. No matter how he pleads to be left alone she will not go. At long last they reach a compromise. He'll live at the top of the hill and she'll stay at the bottom. She readily agrees to this as she is near enough if he ever needs her. Taylor and Grange are delighted to be free at last. They wander together until they come to the land of Eden. It is also a luscious land and here they lay down with wood nymphs. They prosper and multiply to create a just and fair community.

Orpheus is delighted with all the arrangements. The life of a hermit is what he craves. One day, exploring his surroundings, he comes across a slab of white marble. This is exactly what he wants to build an altar to Eurydice. At the top of the hill is a cave, hidden by shrubbery. It's here he places the marble slab. He carves a little seat out of rock and a tiny fireplace. Though small, it's enough for his purpose. A dolman is his bed. One day Enda comes to visit. She dances around Orpheus telling Eurydice she had a dream about ending her days in a white church. Though thrilled to hear this, he insists she is not to come again.

All his needs are fulfilled. Faolain is always at his side. Hens leave eggs outside his cave every morning. Vegetables and fruit grow in abundance. Birds accompany him on the lyre making even sweeter music. Some nights when the moon is full he visits the little people. It's during these times he finds peace of mind. Even Enda, keeping a close watch on him, never discovers where he goes.

Mae Newman

Secrets of the Tower

A disastrous time for the farmers when the flood wiped out their crops and what livestock survived were sickly. A few families had lost everything so people gathered together in the church hall to help. Fintan pledged some grain and a cow. Another farmer gave two of his sheep. Someone else handed out vegetables. Again Fintan stood up; he offered to let people's animals graze on his land which was on the hills of Ballymount. He promised to search for some of the herbs his father spoke of, to make the animals well.

Fintan rose early the next morning and set off up along the dirt track. Past the old Castle Tower until he reached the barn. Taking Hercules the black stallion out of his stall he climbed up on the ploughhorse's back. The giant beast stood seventeen hands high. They rode off towards Kingswood when suddenly the sky turned black as night. Swirling winds and torrential rain made it hard to see.

Fintan jumped down and wrapped the leather strap of the horse's bridle tightly around his hand. Quickly they made their way into the forest. He tied the horse to a branch of a large oak tree. Inhaling the heavy scent of pine as his eyes adjusted to the dim light. As he walked the dry mixture of earth, leaves and twigs crunched beneath his feet. He was about to return to Hercules when he noticed something moving through the foliage. Tiptoeing closer he realised it was a young girl. She wore a daisy chain crown in her golden red hair and had a smile like soft sunshine in spring and her eyes were as green as emeralds against her cream satin dress.

She giggled and beckoned to him before running swiftly along the pathway. He scurried behind; his lungs ached by the time he reached the small clearing. He heard the gentle ringing of bluebells along with the enchanting melody of a flute. The storm had lifted and he could see a crimson glow in the sky above the setting sun. To the left was a cottage with a full moon hovering just above the thatched roof. The fence was covered in rustic brambles and an apple tree by the porch was laden down with red rosy fruit. A candle shimmered in the window and the music was coming from inside. The young girl stood by the door and again beckoned to him. With each step Fintan thought about turning back yet something urged him to go on.

Inside, a man with a silver beard sat on a toad stool playing a flute. His cap and coat were the colour of grass and he tapped his foot on the floor. A raven haired woman sat beside him. She jiggled the bluebells against her long flowing green dress and fairies danced a jig around the room. A soft glow surrounded them; Fintan rubbed his eyes in disbelief. The music stopped and they all stared at him. The old man extended his hand and said.

'I'm Donagh Mor, a thousand welcomes Fintan. Come sit by the fire and drink a warm potion to ease your troubled heart. We know times are hard in your world; and we can restore the balance of nature if you will do this one thing for us. Take this sack of grain with you and leave it by the Round Tower in Ballymount on your way home. For the troops will congregate there from all over Ireland. It's there they replenish their stocks and share out the wealth. Before moving on down through the catacombs to reach the palace near by. Then we can all celebrate the night away at the Tooth Fairies' Ball.

Now put these herbs and nettles in your pocket and make sure you boil them well. Sure a few drops of it in the beast's water will certainly cure their ills. For it 'twas your father who sheltered us from the fairy hunters nearly fifty moons ago. Now we can return the favour one hundred fold. First drink up; enjoy the party for they dance a merry jig. Then young Erin will sing like an angel before she can claim her gossamer wings.'

Fintan couldn't take his eyes off her as she sang a heavenly song. When she had finished, his jaw fell open wide as she shrank down to fairy size. She twirled and squealed merrily as she extended her delicate silk like wings. The others flew about her before hovering in the air. Each one changed colours until a rainbow appeared over her head. His tears of joy were noticed and the old woman gathered every one. She smiled at him and whispered.

'Only soft rain will fall on you from now on,' she said, handing Fintan a bag of gold seeds she'd sprinkled with fairy dust. She added 'Plant them on your return and leave the rest to us.'

She touched his hand with the hazel rod and he fell fast asleep. She bestowed on him thoughts of summer things and of those he loved so much.

When he awoke by the edge of the forest he presumed it had all been a dream. Yet he still held the bag tightly in his left hand. He planted the corn in the field and left the grain by the tower. He looked about and listened out for signs of wee folk on the hill. But all he saw were throngs of daisies dancing in the cool breeze.

The corn grew up overnight and there was plenty for everyone. The fields of Ballymount were extra fertile from that day on. For many years Fintan went back to the forest and swore he heard the sweet melody drifting through the trees. His search was in vain because he never caught sight of the fairies again.

Betty Keogh

Round Tower

I was awakened last night with a feeling of dread and fear, I knew I was being drawn to the Round Tower. It was a chilling feeling because although it had been four years since the Goddess Chalchicue, Goddess of the Tower had summoned me, at that time she told me I had been chosen and that I must wait earnestly for the call.

I left my house and tried to quell the stomach clenching feeling of dread. I decided to cut through St John's Wood, no longer a woodland but land that's now filled by acres of houses. The old rusted gate at the top of the road still hangs upon tired hinges, no longer there to keep the wandering cows within, redundant except for being a gateway to many memories of childhood days. I crossed the stile into Corkagh Park and walked past where Corkagh house once stood within the moat of a castle. It was completely demolished in earlier decades and although there are no features left visible above the ground the aura of that great house is still palpable in the pre-dawn mists that rolled through the park. I passed through the overgrown arch of yew trees and was shrouded once again in darkness as the beech hedge alongside had grown to the height of the tallest trees. I quickened my pace and was relieved to reach the ruins of the old oil and gunpowder mill where the water from Mill Pond gave light as it reflected the moon. Remarkably this pond is unchanged though it exists in the shadow of a new state of the art swimming pool. I stopped for a moment and realised my heart was racing and my breathing unsteady even though my footsteps had slowed as I neared the Tower. Then I felt eyes upon me. I turned and saw that the swans on the pond, regal and poised had cast a curious eye towards me and then as if knowingly, continued their graceful poetic movement across the Mill Pond. Did they know I had been called, had the goddess inspired them, or had my mind become too fanciful? I moved on, the still water of the River Camac filled their pond and held its breath, before it reached the ruins of the old mill and then gushed headlong and noisily to its destination. Finally, I had reached my destination across from the site of the old paper mills where the Mill Shopping Centre now stands, a daily hive of activity, busy shoppers oblivious to the watchful eyes from the Round Tower above them.

On climbing the spiral steps outside and entering the cold stone tower I was stunned to see how displeased the Goddess of the Tower was. She ranted and raved about how selfish and ungrateful the humans had become, her jade green skirt swishing wildly filling the circular room at the top of the tower as she stormed around. The world had become a vicious and unhappy place, she snarled. She stopped now and then to glare out the dark window. Her eyes purple and clouded with grey, a vision of the monsoon she had so long imprisoned deep inside her. 'Do they not realise how their ingratitude enrages us,' she shouted. On and on she went, her madness becoming more and more apparent. The veins in her arms showed the ice that ran through them pooling in the madness that was her mind. She ranted on about the greed of the Zanarconda beings knowing no bounds. The Zanarcondas were the vicious opposing group to the gods and goddesses that protected our lands. They were the lizard headed creatures with tongues filled with deadly venom and tails twice their size. Piercing me with her wild eyes, she unburdened herself of the whole horrifying tale.

The Zanarcondas were working quickly, multiplying at a terrible rate. They had achieved the full metamorphosis to human form so that they could work with, and alongside the real humans, never satisfied and causing untold damage worldwide. They came here, firstly, cleverly disguised as property developers, infiltrating all areas, demolishing the towers of the gods and goddesses around the country and building what they called apartments. These so called apartments were in fact their headquarters. They filled them with their soldiers from all different lands. One group of Zanarcondas tried many times to have her tower razed to the ground but she held firm and had that particular faction destroyed. They had moved too quickly though and had become strong, they had now taken over the leader of the country not caring how blatant the fact that he was in league with them. His recent decision-making alone showed the extent to which they had invaded his mind.

I stood watching her, terrified but at the same time I felt invigorated. I could feel power building inside me as if she was passing it through me as she spoke. 'Don't these humans understand?' she went on, 'to allow my power to be overthrown will result in the end of civilisation and a world under their rule would be a travesty. Already the Zanarcondas have succeeded in devaluing all the currency, they are shutting the country down slowly but surely. Commerce is grinding to a halt. Their power is becoming too great, across the world they have infiltrated our rule and the other gods and goddesses worldwide have given me my instructions. We are to use our individual powers of greatness to solve the situation and this plan is to be set in place immediately.'

She told me to gather five males and five females, no more, and bring them to the Tower, I would have two days and two nights to organise everything. When all was in place she would use her power as Goddess of Water to unleash a mighty flood to destroy this land and all in it, save for the occupants of the tower, who would be spared to begin the new world.

As I left the Round Tower, dawn shed its light over the village, the gothic outline of the church of
The Immaculate Conception etched against the sky, its great body soon to gaze upon the birth of a new world. The blue sky and sunlight belied the tremendous change that was to take place.

Doreen Duffy

Croínn, The Celtic Tree of Knowledge

Local lore informs us Croínn, the Celtic God of Trees and their knowledge came into being in our very own Corkagh demesne, right here in Clondalkin. Croínn (Croíabhann), Croí- heart, Abhann, river, began from the belly of Mona (í-mo-é) nature's mother and MacDara of Timbrelle. In a time when gods were prevalent and not all of them benevolent, some even possessed a darker heart, Croínn was perhaps the kindest of them all. Wise and caring, strong yet gentle were just some of his attributes. Tenacious. Respectful of all. And much was sacred to him. He lived in the forest with the wood nymph Aisling, safe keeper of the Book of Truths and weaver of dreams. And love was ever in the mix. Blended into everything a sun shone high in their hearts. Nature too sang her own celebratory love song.

But not too far away, Mal the malicious miscreant was not so deep in his slumber. Lying low, always keeping an eye out. Ever watchful. Planning to cause a famine of the soul and wreak havoc in Aoife's garden. Spell binder extraordinaire, all evil at his disposal. Forever waiting in the long grass for the opportune moment to strike fear and disharmony into nature's heart, create an imbalance. 'Disharmony', he said, 'was music to his ears'. And he perched high upon the peril and laughed at the danger, the pain he inflicted. Conflict was good. So very, very good. Greed a big spender. Keep them at the trough, gorging on nothing much. Never sated, ill at ease.

Consumerism, drive it down every road. Force-feed them. Let it eat them all up, until they become less than they really are. Make them an enemy unto themselves. Their own shadow-stalking, a threat. And the cruellest of thefts, the theft of themselves. Hook them in at the beginning. Brand them a sinner. Keep them saying they are sorry. Make them pay, forever and ever, amen. Give them a demon, a black knight to torment them, a white knight to save them. A God to believe in. Threaten their freedom. Religion will save the day.

But it is all about the money. The power. The control. The uranium, the lithium, the oil, diamonds and the gold. Stray the indigenous. Push them on to harsh terrain. Badlands. Hope that they sicken and die out. They have the ancient knowledge. They know where the truth lies. It is written on every leaf, on every blade of grass, on every grain of sand. And keep her milking in the parlour. Battered like a hen. Forever bleeding. Her most precious blood be spilt. The Goddess Eve. She is only a woman. Flood her with children. More issues mean more profit. And the man in the big house, the Papa who preaches. It is sheer vanity that got him there. And the card game they play is beggar my neighbour. Politics. Religion. Economics. The not so blessed Trinity. Underneath a sacred oak in Corkagh Demesne, this sacred truth is buried.

Veronica O'Neill

Weeping Willow

The willow dip
Their pendant boughs,
Stooping as if to drink.

-Cowper

My ancestors came from Babylonia an ancient empire of Mesopotamia. Planted along the banks of the Euphrates river, their roots sunk deep into the moist earth, the weeping willow basked in the admiring glances of passers-by. Pendulous leaves created a canopy where tired souls rested, protected from the mid-day sun. Here the willow was sacred to the gods who bestowed many blessings and enchantments on them. However, in Turkey we were a symbol of sadness and were found mainly in burial grounds. It was the same in China, only they believed that the spirits of the dead would become part of the tree and thereby live forever. In Greece we were hailed as the sacred tree of the Gods Hecate and Persephone who were both underworld deities and used the willow for magic. Because of our slender snake-like branches the Druids linked us to the serpent. On St Helena we gave comfort to Napoleon during his exile and when he died he was buried beneath his favourite tree, a weeping willow. Cuttings from this tree became a valued prize among his admirers worldwide.

Napoleon's remains now rest in Paris.

Many legends surround our introduction into Europe. One is that the poet Alexander Pope planted a willow from a twig he got from a Turkish lady, but the truth is we were brought across the sea by traders and flourished in the wet climate. Soon poets and writers began to write about us but they mainly associated us with sorrow and separation.

With a willow in her hand
upon the wild sea banks
and waved her love
to come again to Carthage – Merchant of Venice

I have my roots in Bohernabreena deeply embedded in the damp soil flanking the reservoir. In the beginning I wanted to go back to the humid river margins of the Euphrates. It is said that I can uproot myself at night and stalk travellers but that is not so. As I bent towards the glassy water trailing my slender branches, straining to uproot myself, the supply of moisture had the opposite effect and strengthened my hold on the muddy banks. Over time I had to resign myself to my fate and so I began to take note of my surroundings.

It is a place of beauty and peace here, a region rich in nature. Yellow heather abounds and draws music from the birds while fishermen wait patiently for a bite in the still water. It is a place for people to stroll and dream and comtemplate life's way. Unaware and living within themselves most people pass me by yet some stop to admire my beauty and my grace as I sweep low to create a canopy with my cascading leaves. These are the ones who benefit from my powers of enchantment and dreaming. My connection to the water links me to the Moon Goddess Belili, the willow mother. She granted me the gift of bestowing protection, fertility, love and healing upon those who come to sit beneath my leafy mantle. Their emotions, thoughts and dreams escape into the ground and my enchantment begins to work.

As I draw energy from the soil it seeps into every slender branch which overflows and fills my leaves with a pulsating and lively force. Thus, my abilities remain strong and never wane. If you listen closely you can hear me whisper in the wind as I converse with Belili. Through her I have helped many to overcome their difficulties. Young barren women crying out for life have been fruitful. I have healed those sick in body and soul and given hope to those in mourning. My grace and beauty have inspired peace and comfort in troubled minds. I have touched the spirits of those who murmur secrets beneath my boughs.

In winter, I sleep and dream of the margins of my origins, the impressive Euphrates river. However once spring arrives and the first buds burst forth I stretch out my slim willowy branches and bend down to drink. The Moon Goddess playfully drags the water to and fro making me reach out further each time and thus I become more rooted in the soggy earth. Patiently I wait in the valley for someone to draw close and talk softly to me. In turn I can give hope and inspiration to those who listen closely. I can share the knowledge I acquired since the time of the ancients. I will reveal to you now some of those truths.

We cannot be contained in the past or in the future. They are not containers.
There is no time, everything happens at once.
There is no past nor is there a future, there is just the present moment, ribbons of events unfurling, leading us on and playing us out.
Everything is underfoot, there is no need to look into the distance.
We travel together with everything else on earth around the sun through space.

With the guidance of the Lunar Goddess Belili I will use my powers to give comfort and solace to all who seek me out just as my ancestors have done down through the ages. Pay me a visit some time, you will be surprised.

Joan Byrne

The Wrath of Plagerous

It was with a heavy heart and minus an eye that Parthalon of Greece was exiled because he fought and killed his evil family. Blinded in one eye, he escaped with his beautiful wife, Delgnat, his three sons, their wives and a group of a thousand. They endured an adventurous passage around by Sicily and up towards the Irish Sea, finally landing in Ireland. During his long journey he fought many pirates and plunderers including a tough battle against the Tomorans. He found the ideal place to settle in the area we now know as Tallaght, South Dublin.

The Dublin Mountains made a great lookout for invaders, he could see over a large area right out to the sea. He built some stone and mud huts where his look-outs could shelter while protecting his new realm. In the lower hills he made his first encampment, cut down some of the forest and flattened out the land into a plateau. The trees provided firewood for warmth and cooking. The fertile land provided grasses for his cattle, the first cattle ever in Ireland. In the valley below he could grow things to eat and because he was a great alchemist and had magic powers, he discovered many cures among the wild herbs and flora.

The Parthalons prospered for many years and their numbers increased from a thousand to nine thousand. Their communal dairy farm reached from the Dublin Mountains across what is now Dublin City going north to Howth and west as far as Tara. Parthalon was so happy and all the misery of his past seemed behind him. The group had a great life, they worked hard and played hard, their singing and dancing rocked the area.

During that time Parthalon was devastated on his return from a meeting at Tara, to hear his beloved Delgnat had given herself to a lowly servant. It seems a copious amount of alcohol was consumed by both parties during a celebration while her husband was away. So, he devised a court which would try his wife, find her guilty and decide a punishment for her. The members listened to Delgnat as she weaved her spell, she pleaded her case and told of neglect. As her tears fell and flowed down the mountain they formed a great lake beneath, which became one of the Blessington lakes of today. She beguiled them with her beauty and charm just as she had the unfortunate servant who by now was on his way to Connamara only to be clubbed to death by the Fir Bolg who
didn't take kindly to some Greek invading their strongholds. Nevertheless, Parthalon accepted the decision and vowed to be a more attentive husband.
A few years later thunder roared and lightening flashed across the sky signalling a downpour that lasted three days and nights of complete darkness. Out of a great cloud that lay on top of the mountain, a large fist first emerged followed by a gigantic, hideous body, half man half beast with hooves. When he opened his mouth his teeth resembled that of a giant wolf. His name, Plagarous, breathed a fowl smelling gas over the whole area. People gagged at

the stench and some even vomited. Frantic, Parthalon stoked his fire and stirred his herbal mix, he used all his powers of magic and alchemy as he bellowed his incantations over and over again, echoed by his frightened clan. Exhausted, he fell on his knees calling to Zeus, the all-powerful one but his pleas went unheard or the power of the evil one proved overwhelming. Plague descended on the colony and there was a sudden onset of sickness spreading quickly throughout the area. Dead bodies were piling up all over the place, relatives too sick to bury them. Maniacal laughter was heard in the skies as they fell one after the other until almost the whole population was either dead or dying. The loud wailing, the sight of people in pain, their bodies decaying as they were dying, was terrible to behold. The smell got worse as diarrhoea and rotting corpses added to the breath of Plagerous. Parthalon was one of the last to fall and his dying words were to the gods to spare some of the young to carry on his work. Thuan, son of Parthalon was one of the few to survive the plague. He drowned in a lake that burst forth from the earth and swallowed him up. After Parthalon's death the place where he spent many happy years was named Taimhleacht Mhuin-Tire-Parthaloin.

Today if you wander in the Tallaght hills you may feel a warm breeze on your face or the touch of a shadow passing by. The spirit of Parthalon is still a presence in the place which he loved. He's happy to see another settlement of people prospering on his old patch many centuries later. But are angry gods lurking above planning to wreak havoc again? We have had other plagues in the area every few centuries, might there be one due again?

Brigid Flynn

Hidden

A small girl wanders through the castle grounds, a rag doll swinging in her hand for company. Her hair trails on the soft rolling slopes of the green lawn below. It is summer and Meadhbh her tutor has left, deserting her to her mother and grandmother. No sun pierces through the low fog that obscures the castle behind.
The giant round stone structure blocks her view of the river Dodder to the south. Nearby, horses pull their cargo on the highway. Farmers travel to trade their produce in the village, and families pass by with echoes of laughter on their way to the fair. Grainne imagines she plays with the country children as she moves in circles in the swaying grasses. She dreams that when she is older she will leave this stagnant place, but her mother Caoimhe tells her that this can never be. She is forbidden to trespass the river. The walls and hedgerows are too high for her to climb. She has never been across the boundaries of the castle lands at Rathfarnham.

It is late in the evening when she returns home for dinner. The soldiers who guard the walls do not smile as she passes them on her way to the dinner hall to join her mother. Grainne's grandmother eats alone in quarters in the north tower, so it is only Caoimhe who stares across the table with intensity and watches every morsel Grainne eats on the wooden blocks she insists they use. Caoimhe refuses to use the silver dinner plates despite their wealth.
'Why can't I play with the other children in the

village?' Grainne asks her mother.

'It's not safe there,' Caoimhe replies.

'But Meadhbh says that is not so.'

'Meadhbh does not understand these things.'

'But, please….'

'You cannot go. Let that be an end to it!'

Grainne hangs her head and does not answer.

'Tell me where you played today, my love?' Caoimhe asks her gently.

'In the top meadow,' Grainne whispers, but they remain silent thereafter.

Grainne's grandmother is beautiful. She lives in the battlements that face north. Grainne rarely sees her and only when accompanied by Caoimhe. There is a looking glass in her grandmother's room but it is always covered before they enter. Caoimhe disapproves of this vanity and has locked the rest of the mirrors in the west tower. No one has lived there since the siege years before.

Grainne sees fear in Caoimhe's face as she watches the covered glass behind them. Caoimhe is afraid as she watches the matriarch of this cursed fortress that has passed down through their family for generations. They are what remains, they who hide away from the world.

It is another day. There is thunder and Grainne remains inside, safe from the lightening that flashes around the castle walls. She has wandered to the west tower and sits on the landing on dusty floorboards and examines the threads that make up her doll's face with its black woollen eye stitches, and the heavy strands of dark thread for hair. There is a mirror hanging so high that she cannot even make out the ancient carvings on its frame.

She lies down and sleeps and dreams of her father and brothers. She has seen their images on the painting her mother keeps in their bedroom, but Grainne does not recognize them, they are strangers to her. She and her mother are with them on this canvas, smiling, her mother's expression carefree. Caoimhe has told Grainne that they died when she was very young, but she avoids her daughter's eyes when she tells this story so that Grainne does not believe what she says. But still, she knows that they are dead.

There is a rumble and Grainne wakes. She thinks the mirror moves forward a little but is not sure. She looks but it is still in place and so takes her doll up from the ground. She hears her mother shouting from below. The floorboards beneath her shift and she is confused. Suddenly the mirror slides and moves down the wall, falling to the floor that shudders to support its great weight, until its frame settles against the wall.

The glass has not broken. Grainne raises her eyes and dares to look. Caoimhe is screaming below, straining as she claws her way up the stairs.

'Turn away,' she cries but it is too late, 'get away from there!' She is almost at the landing but Grainne is unable to move. She stares at her reflection for the first time and sees the cold red dress, the doll, her hands, her face, but somehow it is not her. The surface moves as if she is reflected in water. Then her vision clears and she sees herself for the first time.

Now she understands. Her skin is coarse and red. Her eyes are sunken. It is her forehead and nose that are the most horrible to see, until she notices the deepest scar that almost cuts her chin in two. Her mother's hands reach her, her arms crashing past, through the mirror's surface, splintering, bleeding to free her from this sight. Grainne turns away, shivering, hiding her face in the floor as she has been taught to do.

Caoimhe cries and pulls her daughter to her, pushing the mirror over until it smashes underneath the oak panel, until her daughter is safe from its vision of her. She holds her daughter in her arms as Grainne's body shakes. Grainne remembers the siege of the castle, the fire that has killed her brothers, and father, but has left her to live. Her hands cover her open mouth and she cries coloured tears of pain, as her mother's blood slips through her hair, caressing her.

Now she understands why she can never leave.

Vivienne Kearns

From Sherwood to Kingswood

At long last here was something in the distance. Robin raised his hand, placed it on his craggy brow and gazed through the morning mist. 'Hibernia…. Hibernia…..' he cried out. The other members of the crew simultaneously threw their hands towards the sky and roared out with sheer joy–their voices so thunderous that they could be heard by Great God himself.

After two weeks traversing the dangerous waters of the Irish Sea; Robin Hood, Maid Marian, Friar Tuck and Little John had, by some miracle brought their boat to within sight of land. As they approached the shore the sun was lighting up in earnest so the woods of Dun Laoghaire became visible in the distance. At that moment, Robin hoped his host McDara Caol would find them and bring them across the Dublin Mountains and through Tymon Forest and straight on to the Castle at Kingswood. McDara had invited Robin Hood to Ath Cliath to aid the destitute inhabitants. The authorities,both civil and clerical had imposed severe taxes and were harsh on any peasant who could not pay. With a price of many gold coins on his head in England it was a good time for Robin to steal away from Sherwood Forest and turn his hand to aid the poor this side on the water.

As the boat neared the shore Friar Tuck blessed the voyage, blessed the sea, and he blessed the land that they were about to make home. Suddenly terra firma. Hibernia – at last! And now for the wait until McDara Caol would find them. Robin accompanied by his trusty bow and arrow headed for cover as Friar Tuck and Little John waited impatiently for food. Robin did not disappoint them – and returned with a wild pig slung over his shoulder. The fire was lit and soon, the smell of roasting pig was rising up and tantalising the nostrils of the weary travellers. Soon they were tucking in and devouring the beast much to the bewilderment of the onlookers who had gathered on the seashore. Word spread like wildfire about the strange visitors and it came to the ears of McDara Caol and by late evening he and his supporters arrived with the spare horses. It was nightime when they started for Kingswood Castle. The moon poured a yellowy light on the landscape as they slowly made their way over rugged terrain and towards morning they arrived at Belgard Forest and moved south to Kingswood Castle itself. Sleep was the only thing on their minds.

The following morning Robin wasted no time in setting up training camp. He soon had McDara's men in training, instructing them in archery and hand to-hand fighting. Over the next few days McDara and Robin travelled through the fields and woodlands to Clondalkin, Rathcoole and Saggart to familiarise himself with the terrain. The dirt route into Atha Cliath from Nas Na Ri was the prime target – this route was used daily by the wealthy landowners who traded in the Dublin markets. The position of Kingswood Castle was ideal for the business Robin and McDara had in mind – close enough to the route to Dublin and well covered and protected by woodland, shrub and stream. Kingswood Castle itself had a beautiful maze of underground tunnels and escape routes that made it the perfect hiding place.

The day had come when the men were ready for action. Robin placed himself on the hill overlooking the castle and surveyed his men below,'I ask you,' he addressed the men, 'to take this pledge before God and man.Will you always help the poor and needy? Will you honour women? Will you take from the rich?' 'We will, we will,' the men roared back. 'So let the work begin from now,' Robin retorted.

The sun was asleep when Robin and his men took up their positions just outside Rathcoole. Not a sound, not even the crack of a branch was audible as the prey came trundling along - a carriage with four splendid horses accompanied by four outriders on horseback. They were now just a whisper away.

Suddenly all hell broke loose. Four deadly arrows pierced the horsemen and they fell instantly to the ground as Robin's men rushed forward in an all-out assault on the carriage with the blades flashing in the moonlight. The blades soon turned to deep red as they plunged their swords into the occupants of the carriage, killing all instantly. With rapid speed the booty was collected and Robin and his men headed back to the security of Kingswood Castle, well satisfied with their night's rewards. When word reached Dublin the next day the city authorities had their guards out, but Robin and his men were well out of view. The stolen items were hidden in a dungeon in Kilnamanagh, well away from Kingswood Castle. As the men became better trained and more proficient at their work, the robberies became more audacious. Soon the hoard was building up and McDara arranged to have the stolen goods sold off and Robin and his men, dressed as vagabonds distributed the money to the impoverished people of Dublin.

And so the robberies went on and even though the authorities got close on some occasions, they were beaten off by the superior trained men of Robin. By now a fine cohort of trained men was available to McDara and so it was time for Robin, Maid Marian, Friar Tuck and Little John to say farewell to their adopted land.

Jim Archer

Hera

We were heading for Castlekelly by taking the road past Bohernabreena chapel. Then we decided to take the less steep route, as my sister Helen was a little nervous. Entering the Friarstown glen, and following the course of the stream, which flows through it until we met the road, shortly we were to arrive at the little hamlet of Glassamucky situated in the deep dell and sheltered by a grove of trees. The view and sounds were softened by the early lambing sights and smells. Sensing Helen's edgyness on these winding steep roads I pulled in at a lay-by. We photographed a beautiful stainless steel Celtic cross on the brow of a hill overlooking farmlands. This brought back fond memories of our childhood in County Clare. We talked excitedly of the history of the region. Fionn MacCumhaill, the Fianna and surrounding mountains, the slopes of Mount Pelier on the east, the towering heights of Seechon Corrig, Seefingan on the west, while Kippure, the highest mountain in the view, forms the southern boundary of the valley, and the watershed between the basins of the Dodder and the Liffey.

Returning to the road we continued our journey up the valley, me at the wheel and Helen navigating from local maps and notes. We reached a group of attractive slated stone cottages and etched deeply on a roadside rock was 'Cunard', a very pretty little cluster, like a sparkling jewel hidden in the shade deep amongst some tall trees. Up the road, by a half a mile was Castlekelly. Further along, near the confluence of Cot Brook and the Dodder, is Glennasmole Lodge, sheltered by its woods, standing in a picturesque and commanding position at the head of the valley. In former times this house was known as 'Heathfield Lodge.'

The Valley of the Thrushes is such a peaceful place of pleasant pleasures, it was easy to be close and walk with nature, Helen, linked my elbow for support as we walked the stony avenue, carefully avoiding the cohesive mucky puddles on the way to the front door of the Lodge. A side door creaked slowly, then opened to reveal a wizened crouched old man. A croaky old voice called out, ' Tar anseo, tar anseo'. The call was quite persistant, we followed slowly with curiosity, over cobbled stones carefully, as my sister's crutch kept slipping on the moss. I saw her wince in pain, more than once as she gritted her teeth in determination. Her interest was almost herculean which drove her beyond pain and through the shaded doorway into the hovel like sparse room.

The smell was pretty foul, my sister placed her scarf around her nose and mouth. I gulped down the thick acrid glupy stale odour and prayed I would not be ill. The hearth, burning logs and turf was across the room, three sugar chairs lived around the hearth beneath a deep shelf like mantle. On closer inspection I realised it was a sleeper. The small, decrepit, wizened old man filled the corner chair, providing him with a fuller view of his oncoming visitors. We introduced ourselves. He offered no name but proceeded to talk of the Fianna and legends past. We both settled in for a feast of folklore. I offered to make tea, a nod from the old man, was enough to encourage me to keep going. I salted and scalded the cups well, took the boiled blackened kettle from the wrought iron handle and poured it over loose leaf tea in a chipped glazed earthenware teapot to slowly draw, with time.

He talked of the feast Fionn had in Seefin, which means 'the seat of Fionn'. Fionn and the Fianna were supposed to have feasted there after the hunt. The story goes that a beautiful woman appeared on the scene and invited the whole party to a feast, which they gladly accepted, as they were hungry and fatigued. When they had satisfied themselves at the feast a hideous witch from Greece appeared. She wanted Finn to be her husband.We had grown accustomed to the mingling smells of tobacco, turf, logs, smoke and ash. Particles of dust from the concrete floor floating upwards, smells of coddle dampness and mildewed walls. I could almost taste the pungent smells.

'Hera,' my sister asked,'was it Hera?'The old man gazed into the flames as he spoke, the turf flame lit up his tobacco stained skin and glistened on the drool that slowly trickled down the crevice of his cheek and dribbled off his chin to be absorbed into his soggy sweat stenching muffler.

The old man made the connection between the witch from Greece and 'Hera', explaining that it meant, 'Lady', She was known as the 'White Armed Goddess' and was irresistible when she fragranced her body with a lotion so sweet that it filled the whole universe with its fragrance. She cared for her beauty and bathed every year in the spring, 'Canathus as Nauplia,' and renewed her virginity in the mystical waters. The old man explained that trickery was afoot, one cold and winter night. Hera would not respond to Zeus's sexual advances, she fought him off, but he was to return in the guise of a cuckoo bird that appeared to be frozen with the cold. Hera feeling sorry for the bird, warmed it at her breast. Zeus then turned himself back into his normal shape. Poor Hera was raped and forced to cover her shame under the cloak of marriage.

As the eldest daughter of Cronis and Rhea, Zeus was deemed to give her respect. Hera was associated with Zeus's sovereignty and became the chief feminine deity of Olympus. She sat on a golden throne beside her husband and when she entered the congregation of all the gods, they all rose in reverence to her. She was known as the Goddess of Marriage, Queen of the Gods, wife of Zeus. As the first Lady of Olympus she had an extremely difficult temper and was driven to anger by Zeus's infidelities. She had always been filled with hatred and jealousy which kept her in a constant rage. Her vengeance and vindictive nature was taken out on many gods and goddesses.

All these myths and stories were being passed around at the hunt feast, mixed with the mumblings of marriage to Fionn. All were awaiting his response to her, the Greek witch's repeated question, all eyes averted towards Fionn when he declined, we are told, with honour. *After all*, Fionn thought, *if she sided with the Trojans because she lost a beauty contest, well, there would be little hope for loyalty and the years had taken their toll as she could only be described as precious ugly.* 'We are told,' said the old man, that she was so enraged at his refusal, that she told them that she would kill them all. She assembled her fleet and set sail to sea. The old man yawned, and stretched his weary limbs. Several times he rambled in and out of his native spoken Irish. As that was his pleasure we did not interrupt. My sister is fluent and the bits I missed I knew she would have in her notes for me. The woman should have been born with a pen in her hand, she was always writing.

We both shook hands with the old man and left quietly. We ambled along until we came to Fionn's boulder, leaning our backs against the firm coolness drawing strength into the very fibre of our beings, remembering to make a wish.

Maeve Murphy

Contributors' Notes

Jim Archer came to Kingswood via Cork, London and Paris. He started writing at an early age and had his first poem published aged sixteen in Australia. He wrote five stage shows for the Tops competition and won the best script award in Ireland, and co-produced the Ford Motor Company Show. He also won an award for one hour drama in the West Cork Festival in the seventies. He has written poetry,short stories and is now concentrating on the internet where he sees sees the future. He is a blogger - jimarcherscribblerand.com and his humourous novel "RAWMEASHIN" will be published this year.

Niamh Bagnell is a poetry and fiction writer based in Lucan. She hosts a weekly local radio show on writing and reads her work wherever she gets a chance. She has devoted the last 12 years of her life to uncovering the true history of Citywest through meticulous research and presents her findings in this volume in as straightforward and unbiased a fashion as possible.

Joan Byrne has lived in Tallaght for 38 years. 'I love to write, especially about the surreal and the magic of life in which we are all immersed but are often too busy with everyday living to see. My interests stem from my time spent in Maynooth College where I studied Spanish literature and philosophy.'

Eileen Casey facilitates creative writing courses in adult education, Old Bawn Community School, Tallaght and Kilroy's College, Home Tuitions. Twice short listed for a Sunday Tribune Hennessy Award, her debut poetry collection *Drinking the Colour Blue* (New Island) was published in 2008. Other publications include, *Reading Hieroglyphs In Unexpected Places* and *The Jane Austen Sewing Kit. From Spit and Clay* won the 2010 Green Book Festival Award, Los Angeles (poetry category). She has shown three poetry in public places solo exhibitions, 'Reading Fire, Writing Flame' was awarded by Offaly County Council, 2006 and featured in *Poetry Ireland* (Issue No. 92) and *The Irish Arts Review* (Spring, 2008).

Susan Condon, writer and poet, lives in Dublin with her husband and two children. She was recently awarded 1st prize for her short story, "The Visit", in The Sports and Cultural Council - City of Dublin VEC Short Story Competition. She successfully completed creative writing courses in Old Bawn Community School, adult education and is a member of Platform One, Rua Red.

Ann Cullen is an American citizen who moved to Ireland and settled in Tallaght with her new husband, a native Dubliner. Her educational background includes Classic and Contemporary Irish Literature and Native American Studies. She also attended, and enjoyed, creative writing classes in Old Bawn Community School adult education. Recently relocated to Nevada, she is currently writing short stories inspired by her experiences living in magical South Dublin.

Robert Dowdall: 'After losing my sight due to a car crash in Sept.'89 my path became somewhat twisted and bumpy until I finally found my passion for alternative medicine in which now I practise in a variety of therapies and also teach yoga. My latest passion is creative writing and, like the alternative medicine, it is up-lifting and liberating.' Robert, after climbing Mount Kilimanjaro, began writing in 2009 upon completing enjoyable creative writing courses in Old Bawn Community School, adult education.

Doreen Duffy lives in Clondalkin. A busy mother of three, being placed in the South Dublin County Council Creative Writing Competitions ,The Jonathan Swift Writing Awards and the City of Dublin VEC Creative Writing Awards gave her the impetus to continue. She completed a number of creative writing courses in Old Bawn Community School.

Brigid Flynn, originally from Kells, Co. Kilkenny, has lived in Tallaght since 1976 and is a member of St Muirin's Writing Group since the mid 90's. Also a member of Platform One, Red Rua, she has been successful in many local writing competitions including The Francis Ledwidge, The Jonathan Swift and South Dublin Council's Social Inclusion Week, 2009. Her hobby as a slogan writer won her many prizes including winning *Barry's Tea Dream Escape* prize of a €5000 holiday voucher in 2003.

Marie Gahan is a native Dubliner. Poet, fiction writer and journalist, her work has been published in outlets such as New Irish Writing, among others. In 2008 "Meemaw" was shortlisted for The William Trevor Short Story Prize. In 2009, her winning poem at Listowel Writers' Week, became the title for her debut poetry collection *The Margarine Eaters* from Lapwing . A founder member of St Colmcille's
Writers' Group, she is a V.E.C. Tutor and facilitates St Muirin's Writing Group, Avonbeg, editing *Flower Gathering*, the group's debut anthology. In October, 2010, on the invitation of Amergael, she will read her work on a reading tour of America.

Genevieve Greene is a native Dubliner and came to live in Tymon North, Tallaght, with her husband Tony thirty-one years ago. She has four daughters and one grand-daughter. A member of St Murin's Writing Group since 2000, she enjoys reading and writing. Writing is a compulsion, when an idea takes seed she just lets it flow and never knows where it will go.

Vivienne Kearns was short listed for the Fish Short Story Competition 2010 with a version of this story, also entitled "Hidden". Vivienne has produced and presented three Arts shows for Radio Tallaght in 2009 and is a member of the Platform One, Rua Red. She was also short listed for the Bibliofemme short story competition in 2005 with "Lost Gamines". Vivienne has travelled extensively, and has lived in the US and the UK. She is currently working on her first novel.

Colm Keegan lives in Clondalkin, Dublin. He writes poetry, short stories and screenplays. He's currently working on a novel and his first poetry collection. He runs Nighthawks, Dublin's premier arts night, and is an arts reviewer for RTE radio. He has no idea what he's doing, and has been doing it for years.

Betty Keogh is a true Dubliner. She is married with two grown-up children and lives in Walkinstown. She began writing several years ago in a creative writing course facilitated by Marie Gahan in Greenhill's College. In 2005, her poem 'New Year Wish' appeared in *Paint the Sky with Stars*, an anthology of Tsunami poems published by Reinvention, UK, in aid of the disastor fund. She was highly commended for her fiction in the inaugural Jonathan Swift Awards, Saggart.

Brian Kirk lives in Clondalkin, Dublin. He was shortlisted for Hennessy Awards in 2007 and 2010, and Over The Edge New Writer of the Year Awards in 2008 and 2009. He won the inaugural Writing Spirit Award in 2009. His work has appeared in The Sunday Tribune, The Stony Thursday Book, Crannog, *Revival* and various anthologies.

Julie Coombes Kiernan is originally a northsider but moved to Kilnamanagh, Tallaght with her husband and five children over thirty years ago. In St Muirin's Writing Group, she discovered the pleasure of writing, especially her memoirs. In 2006, "No Women Allowed in the Cuckoo's Nest" was published in *County Lines: A Portrait of a County* (New Island), edited by Dermot Bolger.

Aine Lyons, is a member of St Muirin's Writing Group. She has lived in historic Tallaght for forty years where the Wicklow mountains are a feast for the eye in every season. Under their spell a cosmic mix of ghosts and goblins spring to life, and strange gods inhabit our space. Her greatest pleasure is crafting poems, especially about nature. Aine's work has appeared in many anthologies, most recently Dermot Bolger's *Night & Day* (New Island) in which he created twenty-four hours in the life of Dublin City. In 2009, her poetry was shortlisted in 'Poetry on the Lake', Italy, adjudicated by Carol Ann Duffy.

Ailish Massey is a retired teacher who has been involved in developing methods of educating deafblind children in Scotland, England and Ireland. She lives in Ballymore Eustace, Co Kildare. She first began work on 'Saved by the Bell' when completing a creative writing course in Old Bawn Community School.

Joe McKiernan: Born in Walkinstown, Joe attended Crumlin CBS and in 1994 began a period of living and working abroad. He has worked in England, The Netherlands and Australia. *Here's To The Primary Colours*, his first novel, tracks the experience of three people who travel to Australia. He enjoys writing in several genres, including science fiction, fantasy, humour and drama. He is also a member of Lucan Writers' Group.

Geraldine Mills has published three collections of poetry and two of short stories. She is the Millennium winner of the Hennessy/Tribune New Irish Writer Award. Her most recent collection of poetry *An Urgency of Stars* (Arlen House) was awarded a Patrick and Katherine Kavanagh Fellowship. She is currently working on a collaboration of poetry with American poet Lisa C. Taylor.

David Mohan prefers myths to facts, and fairy tales to spin. In his head he lives in Lucan, but also, sometimes, in Paris, Rio and C16th Italy. He prefers sheep in wolves clothing to the opposite and would choose a forest over a housing estate every time.

Grace Moore: 'A native of Belfast, I've been living in Dublin for ten years and in Tallaght for four. As a keen hiker I was inspired to write my Tallaght myth after catching glimpses of deer whilst walking in the Dublin hills, visible from all over Tallaght. Over the years, I've attended creative writing classes in Old Bawn Community School.'

Victoria Mullen lives in Tallaght and runs her own tax consultancy practice. Despite the pressures of work and family life, she decided to take up writing earlier this year by completing a creative writing course in Old Bawn Community School, adult education. 'Red Sky' is her first published work.

Tom Myp is an Irish citizen (at last!) who appeared on these shores several times and in several guises before his final attempt at life without equivocation: he loves Ireland more than anywhere else in the world, and, despite his propensity to slag the people who live here, hopes to live the rest of his life among the denizens of this island.

Mae Newman was born in Clones, Co. Monaghan and now lives in Rathfarnham beside the Hermitage. She is a member of St Muirin's Writing Group and has won numerous prizes for her poetry and short stories. Her debut poetry collection, *Mist Shrouds The Morning*, is due out from Lapwing later this year.

Veronica O'Neill is a Clondalkin poet and writer who regularly attends Clondalkin Adult Morning Education. She has previously published work in *Flavours of Home (*Fiery Arrow Press*)* an anthology of family memories/ /recipes supported by The Social Inclusion Unit, South Dublin County Council.

Louise Phillips, a local historian from South Dublin County, has been an active member of Lucan Writers Group for the last four years. A number of her short stories and poems have been published in anthologies. In 2008 her micro fiction story "The Beads", was published as one of the winning entries in the National Group Writers Award (*Petals on a Bough*) and her short story "A Part of Me" was shortlisted for the Molly Keane Memorial Award. In 2009 her short story "Last Kiss" was the winning entry in The Jonathon Swift Award in Saggart. Louise is now working on her second novel.

Maeve Murphy lives in Clondalkin. She is a Special Needs Classroom Assistant in Old Bawn

Community School where she also enjoys creative writing classes. An inveterate traveller, she is a citizen of the world. Her first published poem appeared in a recent *Riposte* Poetry Broadsheet.

Joan Power lives in Rathcoole with her husband, Jim. She writes a little everyday, sometimes falling off the edge of reason while finding new tribes to belong to, and strange lands to inhabit. The understanding of her family, the friendship of her writing group, St Muirins, and the occasional success in short story competitions, keeps her (mostly) grounded.

Martin Shannon lives in Old Bawn, Tallaght. Since 2006, although wheelchair bound following an accident, he still attends events he previously enjoyed, football and boxing in particular and more recently, creative writing classes in Old Bawn, Adult Education. His writing has appeared in *The Irish Wheelchair Association's Journal.*

Patricia Verdon: 'I discovered my love of writing when I joined an evening class in Old Bawn Community School, facilitated by Eileen Casey, in 2008. Since then I have become a member of Platform One, Rua Red and Virginia House Writers' Group, Rua Red, facilitated by Maria Wallace. I have taken a Platform One Script Writers' Course with Tracy Ryan and enjoyed the experience of hearing my work being read by professional actors. I am also a member of the Bonn Bonn Book Club in Blessington. I have lived in Tallaght since 1983, with my husband and three children.'

Tríona Walsh is a member of Lucan Writers' Group. She has been writing since her teens and has been happily toiling over a novel for the past couple of years. She writes short stories for the instant gratification and to remind herself that she can actually finish something. Tríona won the 2008 Jonathan Swift Short Story competition. She was recently shortlisted for the Malahide Library Short Story Competition and of recent times is part of *The Poetry Divas*, a performance based poetry group who appear regularly at major arts festivals throughout the country.

Acknowledgements are due to:
EBS Community Fund, celebrating 75 years in the community.
South Dublin County Libraries.
Mayor Eamonn Maloney, who is always supportive of local writers and creative endeavours.
Guest Writer Geraldine Mills.
Susan Condon, for her invaluable skill with proof-reading the manuscript.
Tony Fegan, Director, Tallaght Community Arts Centre, Rua Red.
Platform One, Rua Red.
Radio Tallaght, Rua Red, who broadcast some of the work included here in a programme *Re-Imagining South Dublin Landscape*, September, 2009.
Sile Coleman, Local Studies, County Library, Tallaght.
David Mohan for title ideas.
Jim Fitzpatrick (www.jimfitzpatrick.ie) for use of cover images. *Tallaght Village, 2010,* is courtesy of the editor.
The Achill Heinrich Böll Association where the final edits for South of the County, *New Myths and Tales* were carried out.
Abiding respect and gratitude for the commitment of all the writers included in this anthology.
Proceeds from the sale of this anthology will go to Old Bawn Community School, adult education and Platform One, an open forum for writers and artists, Rua Red Arts Centre, Tallaght.